Folk Art
Woodcarving

DATE DUE

DEMCO 38-297

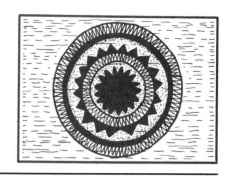

Folk Art
Woodcarving
823 Detailed Patterns

Alan & Gill Bridgewater

 Sterling Publishing Co., Inc.   New York

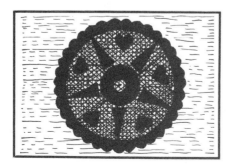

A special thank-you must go to our sons Julian and Glyn for their patience and
for all the tea and biscuits. Thank you, guys.

Library of Congress Cataloging-in-Publication Data

Bridgewater, Alan.
    Folk art woodcarving : 823 detailed patterns / by Alan & Gill
Bridgewater.
       p.   cm.
    Includes index.
    1. Wood-carving—Patterns. 2. Folk art—Europe—Themes, motives.
3. Folk art—United States—Themes, motives. I. Bridgewater, Gill.
II. Title.
TT199.7.B742   1990
736'.4—dc20   90-9963
                                               CIP

10 9 8 7 6 5 4 3 2 1

© 1990 by Alan & Gill Bridgewater
Published by Sterling Publishing Company, Inc.
387 Park Avenue South, New York, N.Y. 10016
Distributed in Canada by Sterling Publishing
c/o Canadian Manda Group, P.O. Box 920, Station U
Toronto, Ontario, Canada M8Z 5P9
Distributed in Great Britain and Europe by Cassell PLC
Villiers House, 41/47 Strand, London WC2N 5JE, England
Distributed in Australia by Capricorn Ltd.
P.O. Box 665, Lane Cove, NSW 2066
Manufactured in the United States of America
All rights reserved
ISBN 0-8069-5746-8

Contents

Preface

This book is a source manual that draws its inspiration from all types of naïve, individual American and European woodwork. By this we mean that we have selected our designs from ordinary utilitarian, uninhibited woodwork that is usually described as being "of the people," or folk art.

This book, therefore, is about those patterns, designs, motifs, and forms that reflect innocence, naïveté, individuality, and the common man. They include swiftly carved lines that run straight and true, softly painted forms that flow in long lazy curves, hard-edged compass-worked circles, chip-carved designs in dizzying spirals, whittled knots that seem endless, inlay flowers, and all manner of tendrils, petals, birds, beasts, and people.

The many woodwork designs have been collected from sources as far apart in time and space as nineteenth-century Pennsylvania and sixteenth-century Transylvania, eighteenth- and nineteenth-century England, Germany, Russia, and New England, and many other places. For easy accessibility, we have organized the designs and motifs into primary pattern-related groups. If you are looking for designs with circles, or plants or whatever, all you have to do is zip through the corner-page "flip" symbols to find your special area of interest.

And if you are looking for basic, naïve, vigorous designs that typify European and American folk art woodwork at its best, then this is the book for you.

1. Wales—love spoon detail; knife-worked, pierced, fretted, and chip-carved (nineteenth century).

2. America—dower chest detail; painted (early nineteenth century).

3. America—whirligig; fretted, painted, and assembled; "card players" detail (nineteenth century).

1

2

3

Introduction

What Is Folk Art Woodwork?

Where does one draw the line between "simple" work produced by the folk artist and "finer" work produced by professional artists and craftspeople? Our distinction has to do, in the main, with the individual woodworkers' view of themselves. In the context of this book at least, folk art woodworkers were ordinary folk, your ancestors and mine, who in artistic innocence made and decorated objects without being affected by styles, trends, or training.

For the purposes of this book, the term "folk artist" has to do with the state of mind of the artist—the key words being "innocent" and "naïve." Folk art woodwork by its very definition is unpretentious; if it is too sophisticated, or if it is overly self-conscious, then it ceases to be folk art and becomes something else. This does not imply that the folk artists were unskilled or that their woodwork was (or is) in any way "low art" or that the artifacts they made were of an inferior nature. Folk art woodwork shouldn't be compared with so-called fine woodwork, but rather should be thought of within its own unique context.

We have been asked why, when we were searching out patterns, designs, and motifs, we looked towards folk art woodwork as opposed to "fine" period woodwork. Our view was (and is) that if the aim is to search out primary woodwork designs, meaning genuinely uncluttered designs, then it follows that we need to consider woodwork that is by its very nature honest and uncluttered. We need to go back to our preindustrial past, to a time when every man was able to clear his own patch of land, to build his own house, to make his own furniture, and to generally beautify his own environment.

There are carved wood, stencilled wood, wooden toys, rough-hewn slab-wood

1. America—stencil detail; (nineteenth century).

2. England—Little Morton Hall Cheshire, detail of framed building (sixteenth century).

1

2

furniture, wood for houses, wood for tools, signs, boxes, chairs, chests, love tokens, and decoys. Wood has always been, in all its many and wonderfully varied forms, man's primary natural raw material.

It was not in his nature for the self-taught folk art woodworker to turn to any professional or specialist for help. He did no more—he could do no more—than to look to his basic tools, to his local wood, to his palette of raw colors, and to all the everyday objects around him.

Certainly there did come a time towards the end of the nineteenth century when many folk art woodworkers did copy trade catalogues, did look to instruction books for ideas, and worked in organized "arts and crafts" communities. But in the main, they were individuals on their own who simply drew inspiration from their cultural and geographical environment.

And so it was that these ordinary untrained folk made and decorated their world: beds and chairs, tables and chests, toys and shop signs, weather vanes and fireboards, and just about every other household object in sight. They painted, carved, stencilled, whittled, drilled, fretted, pierced, and scratched, until the objects that they made were a riot of pattern and color. They didn't think too much about whether or not a specific design was good or fashionable; they simply decorated their woodwork in the many ways they had personally discovered.

3. Germany—toy figures; lathe- and knife-worked, turned, whittled, and carved (late nineteenth century).

4. America, Cobb Island, Georgia—robin snipe decoy; knife-worked, whittled in the round, and painted (nineteenth century).

5. America—weather vane, rooster; saw- and knife-worked, fretted, and painted (nineteenth century).

3   4

5

9

Northern Europe

Sweden

Sweden, a land of trees, is a woodworker's paradise. Until the beginning of the nineteenth century, it was a rural society that in many ways was almost completely wood oriented. The houses were made of massive timbers; they were beautifully built structures with huge carved beams and rafters extending from the low walls up to the ridge pole. The furniture was bold and sturdy; there was a wide range of generously proportioned pieces of woodwork: massive built-in cupboards, long benches, enormous slab-wood tables, slab-back chairs, stools, and much more. And of course, nearly all the woodwork was lavishly carved, brilliantly painted, and otherwise intricately decorated. The houses themselves, the furniture, and the smallest domestic items were all of a piece, in that they evoked an array of wonderful patterns.

Swedish folk art woodworkers—which once meant all the male members of a family—favored knife and gouge techniques that drew on much older traditions. As late as the early nineteenth century, it was still apparent that a great number of old and even ancient designs, patterns, and motifs had survived. Many of the designs are clearly Gothic, Romanesque, and even Viking in origin.

In terms of pattern, design, and motif, Swedish folk woodwork is a unique treasure house of inspiration. In fact, there is so much woodwork, so many wonderful, exciting examples, that it is almost impossible to pick out a single item or style and say that this shape or that form is most popular, most common, or even typically Swedish. Having said that, we feel that in very general terms Swedish folk woodwork can be characterized by three primary items: the huge clothes chests; the small, rather delicate chip-carved love spoons; and the actual houses themselves.

Traditionally the houses were of the log cabin type, the whole structure being built from massive, interlocking, squared-off tree trunks. The ceilings, walls, and floors were all lined out and panelled with split-slab planks.

Characteristically there were two large rooms and a hall, entered through a low and wide main door. Within, there were lines of wooden pegs around the walls, a massive fireplace with a built-in oven, built-in cupboard-type beds that one stepped up to from the floor, and a large central slab table. All the woodwork was, to a greater or lesser extent, generously carved and decorated with chip-carved roundels, borders of twined designs, and running patterns of intricate incised knots.

1. Sweden—chest detail; painted (nineteenth century).

2. Sweden—spoon detail; knife-worked, incised (nineteenth century).

3. Sweden—crown rail detail; knife- and gouge-worked, pierced, carved, and incised (eighteenth century).

1

2

3

Although there were many varied pieces of furniture, from benches and stools to beds and cupboards, we consider the huge boxes or chests as being the most important, the most archetypal pieces of furniture. Because all members of a household kept their personal clothes and effects in their own personal chests, the chests were carved and decorated with distinctive care, flair, and style. And most of the chests have survived. As they did with the house interiors, the chest carvers favored chip-carved roundels, scratched six-point circles, and twined borders.

Although individual folk woodworkers and village groups made a great range of small domestic items—such as dishes, bowls, boxes, food stamps, hanging shelves, chairs, stools, and clock cases—it is the small, beautifully carved and decorated love spoons that seem to us to exemplify the Swedish folk art style. Carved and whittled by lovelorn lads as courting gifts, these spoons can be seen now as wonderful expressions or tokens of love. Using close-grained woods, like yew, birch, white pine, spruce, and sycamore, most country lads would, sooner or later, set out in earnest to carve the most uninhibited, extravagant, and intricate symbols of love. Characteristically, Swedish love spoons are basically spoonlike in shape and decorated with all manner of fanciful chip-carved and incised patterns. These include hearts, magic circles, twined knots, and interlaced lines, as well as dates, names, initials, and personal intimacies that might be exchanged between lovers. Just about every surface is decorated and embellished with symbolic designs and motifs.

One factor that makes Swedish folk woodwork especially exciting is that the styles and techniques shown here lasted in an unbroken tradition from earliest times right through to the end of the nineteenth century.

Norway

Norway is a country of forests, and Norwegian folk have always considered wood to be their primary art and craft material. The wonderful thing about Norwegian folk woodwork is that, through the end of the nineteenth century, there was a healthy, vibrant, living tradition that could easily be traced back to Viking times. This survival of ancient working methods is borne out by the fact that many eighteenth- and nineteenth-century woodworking techniques—the joinery, the carving, and the painted designs—are almost indistinguishable from those used by the old Viking shipbuilders and the medieval church carvers and decorators. This is not to say that latter-day Norwegian folk art woodworkers were in any way copyists or had one eye slavishly on the past. Rather it attests to the fact that the old woodworking traditions were a vital and flourishing part of everyday life.

Norwegian designs and patterns found unique expression in the decorative style known as rosemaling, or rose painting. Rosemaling had its roots in mid-sixteenth-century Norway, when folk artists began to tentatively decorate their furniture and interiors with rather restrained and stylized flowers. From these timid beginnings, the rosemaling technique gradually grew, changed, and developed, until it reached its peak in the middle of the eighteenth century. By then most of the furniture and

4. Sweden—drinking bowl with dragon's head handle; knife- and gouge-worked, stave-built, pierced, and incised (nineteenth century).

5. Sweden—detail from a hanging cupboard; painted (eighteenth century).

6. Sweden—detail from a box; knife-worked, chip-carved (nineteenth century).

4

5

6

interiors were awash with huge, brilliantly colored, unrestrained garlands of brush-worked flowers.

At its best, rosemaling is characterized by the stylized and symmetrically balanced rose-and-tulip flowers-in-vase groups that can be seen on the smaller mid-nineteenth-century chests, boxes, and bowls. The rosemaling tradition lasted throughout the nineteenth century, and then, just as it had slowly grown and developed, so the use of the technique shrank, wilted, and faded. Finally, it lost favor as a style, and was considered only suitable for dower chest decoration.

Denmark

The Danish people have a great and flourishing tradition of folk art woodwork: heavily beamed houses, painted dower chests, beds, massive slab-wood tables, benches, and much more.

Danish woodworkers excelled in the making of chairs, domestic wares, and a particular type of carved and pierced alcove board. These were characteristically pierced and carved boards that were a swirling, waving mass of intricate loops, arches, and stylized plantlike fronds. Of course, both the chairs and the boards are a treat to the eye, and both might equally be chosen as characteristic. But best of all, we like the small, wonderfully carved, intricately fretted, and chip-decorated kitchen and keeping room wares—the love token beaters and mangle boards.

For decorative purposes, these love token boards are very special; they are literally covered in carved patterns, forms, repeats, and motifs. Typically, just about every available surface is decorated with swirls of pattern—everything from sunlike rosettes, twined hearts and tulips, to roses, angels, beasts, birds, dates, and initials.

In comparing these boards, the designs might be thought of as being overly uniform. This is deceptive, for within this seemingly standard uniformity the range of pattern detail is quite amazing. If you are interested in strong, geometrical forms, such as compass-worked rosettes, six-point stars, and the like, then Danish mangle board designs will be of special interest to you.

Iceland

Iceland lies in the Atlantic, just south of the Arctic circle. It's a large, sparse, rocky ocean-island, a dramatic land of volcanoes, glaciers, heaths, waterfalls, and fogs. Iceland is a country that has come over the last 1,000 years to be gradually colonized by the Vikings, Germans, Celts, Laplanders, and Finns.

Iceland is poor in basic woodcraft materials. It has a few native birch trees, and that's about it. This sparseness has encouraged a style of folk woodwork that is uniquely Icelandic. Although in broad general terms the designs and motifs have quite obviously drawn their inspiration from, say, Viking and Danish forms, it is also true that those styles and forms have been reshaped to meet severe Icelandic

1. Norway—detail of lid; painted (nineteenth century).

2. Norway—detail of a bowl handle; knife-worked, whittled, and painted (nineteenth century).

3. Denmark—washing beater detail; knife-worked, chip-carved, incised, and painted (eighteenth century).

1

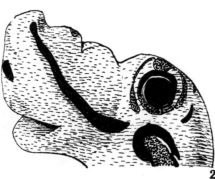

2

3

conditions. For example, because most of the wood had to be imported, furniture traditionally tended to be small and simple. If a house had a bed, a table, a few chairs, and a chest for each member of the family, it was considered to be well furnished. Consequently, although many of the designs, patterns, and forms are Viking, Swedish, Danish, and the like, they have evolved and been reused in unique ways. The Icelandic woodworker didn't consciously take and use, say, a dragon motif from a Viking longship and knowingly adapt it for a bed board. Rather, the designs were slowly changed, reused, and absorbed over many centuries. Traditional designs are now to be found in miniature on bed boards and wood boxes. They are more or less the same ancient designs, but are now used in completely different ways.

4. Iceland—detail from a box; knife- and gouge-worked, carved in relief, and incised (eighteenth century).

5. Iceland—detail from a hand mangle; knife- and gouge-worked, carved in the round, and incised (eighteenth century).

6. Iceland—detail from a cupboard door; knife- and gouge-worked, carved in deep relief with undercuts (seventeenth century).

4

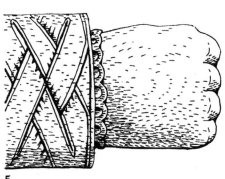

5

6

13

Eastern Europe

Poland

In terms of folk art woodwork, Poland is, perhaps questionably, in the fortunate position of being one of the few countries in Europe to still have a living tradition. We qualify this statement because to some there appears to be a linkup between surviving folk art and economic backwardness. Artistic factors aside, it is thought by many that if a community makes its own chairs or carves its own kitchen wares, then that community is likely to be technologically backward or deprived.

The accuracy of that assumption notwithstanding, many of the isolated areas in Poland do still have a folk woodwork tradition. At least until the late 1960s, wooden houses were still being built. In addition, many of the architectural details were commonly hand-carved, toys and small domestic wares were being made in the home, and so on. The difference is that though many Polish folk art woodworkers do still carve wood, make chairs, paint chests, and the like, now, in the main, such work has become a secondary way of making money.

In our search for strong, vigorous forms and motifs—patterns and designs that can truly be described as being characteristically Polish—we need to begin with the eighteenth and nineteenth centuries. We need to go back to a time when, as a matter of course, woodwork was either made in the home or was crafted by local folk woodworkers. During this period, house beams were carved and incised with huge compass-worked roundels, chests were painted with running swags of brightly colored flowers, cupboards were deeply carved and pierced. Everything was an object of decoration.

Characteristically, just about all the pre-twentieth-century folk woodwork is vigorous and strongly patterned with bold geometrical designs. Compass-drawn circles, pierced borders, and deep chip-carved motifs abound. If you want to go straight to the heart of Polish folk woodwork, the best examples are the scratch-carved chests, pierced-back stick-leg chairs, and spoon racks of those two centuries.

1. Poland—gable end on house; saw- and gouge-worked, cut, fretted, carved, and painted (nineteenth century).

2. Poland—detail from a house ceiling; painted (nineteenth century).

3. Poland—spoon rack detail; knife-worked, pierced, and carved (eighteenth century).

Hungary

Hungary has a very strong woodworking tradition. Low single-story houses with beams, window shutters, doors, and wooden pillars are uniformly made of wood

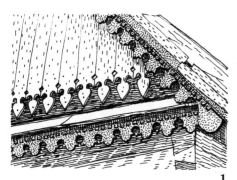

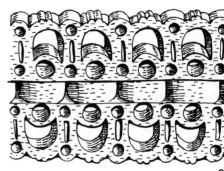

1

2

3

and gloriously carved with folk art motifs, designs, and patterns. Their furnishings—beds, benches, plate racks, chests, and all the usual small wares of everyday living and working—are also made of wood and generously carved, whittled, painted, and otherwise decorated with flowers, compass-drawn roundels, realistic imagery, and geometrical motifs.

In their overall design techniques, it's apparent that Hungarian folk artists have been strongly influenced by Eastern patterns and forms. The designs seem to have drawn their inspiration from Turkey and the Orient, rather than from, say, Germany, France, or the Low Countries.

Of course, with such a wealth of material it's almost impossible to pick one particular technique or form as being representative or fundamentally Hungarian. However, all things considered, we have concluded that Hungarian folk art woodwork is best characterized by two forms, or areas: the small chip-carved items made by shepherds and the delicately carved wood and wax/intarsia wares made in the late nineteenth century by Trans-Danubian herdsmen. The intarsia or wax inlay wares are especially exciting, with the patterns being variously cut away and lowered, and their resultant low relief areas or holes being filled in with colored wax. The designs have a wonderfully exotic Eastern flavor—more like delicate paintings or enamels than inlays.

Such wares and designs are usually worked on small square and oval boxes. They can be recognized by the highly patterned, sharp-edged designs and motifs: couples drinking and smoking, top hats, big capes, lots of zigzag borders, bunches of tulips, and geometrical patterns—all worked in red and dark-blue sealing wax.

Romania

Romania has a strong, vital, and flourishing folk art woodworking tradition. This tradition, it is boasted, goes back at least 2,000 years. From the rugged northern mountain regions to the soft southern plains, there are many contrasting folk art styles and forms. Nevertheless, there is, within this apparent diversity, an overall sameness or uniformity of style and pattern that is uniquely Romanian.

In the mountain regions, for example, the houses are well timbered, and the beams, doors, and window shutters have been variously worked with all manner of geometrical designs and figurative animal carvings. By contrast, in the hill country many of the internal and external boards—roof boards, gable boards, and shelf fronts—are decorated and embellished with pierced flower motifs and running patterns.

But the Romanian folk art styles and forms are a bit deceptive. At first glance it might be thought that, say, the chip carving in Oltenia is quite different from the wonderfully intricate pillar carvings of some of the mountain houses. However, on closer examination, it is apparent that there is a common vein, or core, running through the designs, patterns, and techniques that stamp all these seemingly diverse folk art forms as Romanian. The same can be said of the house interiors, although from region to region the design forms seem to be very different. For example, in

4. Hungary, Trans-Danubia—mirror cover detail; wax intarsia/inlay (nineteenth century).

5. Hungary—mirror back detail; wax intarsia/inlay (nineteenth century).

6. Romania—two slab-back chair details; saw- and knife-worked, pierced, and carved (nineteenth century).

4   5   6

15

the mountains the rooms are beamed and panelled, while in the south the walls are decorated with lots of painted plaster work. But what might easily be missed is that there is a strong overall theme. The house interiors, the furniture, the room plan, and the woodwork patterns and motifs are all of a piece.

In almost every traditional home the kitchen furniture is grouped around the characteristically painted stove and oven. The painted dower chest holds pride of place by the bed, the carved and pierced wall shelves run round the walls, pierced slab-back chairs are around the table, and there might be a heavy bench or two. All the furniture is generously decorated with every technique from chip carving and scratch carving to poker work, piercing, and painting.

As to the techniques, designs, and patterns that might best be described as being characteristically Romanian, it's undeniable that the carved and pierced slab-back chairs are exceptional, and the various small boxes and chest have a wonderful boldness. But perhaps the most uninhibited and exciting patterns and designs are the many small chip-carved domestic wares. There are wonderfully carved and pierced distaffs; brightly painted and scratch-carved loom rods; carved spoons with intricate chip-carved roundels; and beautifully decorated cheese presses, washboards, beaters, breadboards, and nutcrackers.

If your special folk woodwork interest is in small scratch-carved and chip-carved designs, with compass-drawn circles, six-point stars, small flower designs, and the like, Romanian kitchen and hall wares will delight you.

Bulgaria

The Bulgarian woodworking tradition employs two main forms of decorative carving: scratch carving, or incised work, and deep-gouge carving.

There is a great deal of large house deep-gouge carving—wall panels, doors, cupboards, and the like—but most of this work is done by professional woodworkers, with one eye on fashion and the other on profit. So it must therefore be acknowledged that this type of woodwork falls a little outside the folk art tradition.

Bulgarian scratch-carved, or incised, design is found on most everyday common or garden domestic wares—boxes, washing boards and beaters, distaffs, shepherds sticks, and so on. The folk art carvers favor simple naïve designs and patterns: compass-worked circles, zigzags, lines and squares, stars, cross-hatching, stylized hearts, and flowers. Items and objects to be decorated are very often built-up, carved in the round, painted, and then scratch-carved.

1. Romania—dower chest detail; painted (nineteenth century).

2. Bulgaria—plate detail; turned, patterned with a hot poker, and painted (nineteenth century).

3. Bulgaria—shepherd's staff detail; knife-worked, carved in the round, and chip-carved (nineteenth century).

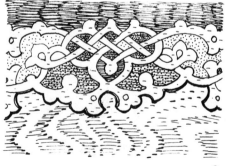

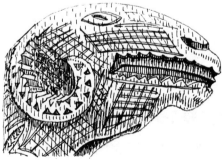

1   2   3

Southern Europe

Yugoslavia

Yugoslavia is a country that has seen many invasions and migrations. It is a mixing pot, a coming together of styles, peoples, customs, and cultures. The Turks, Greeks, Austrians, and Russians, the Romans and the Byzantines, have all, at one time or other, influenced the folk art woodwork of the many small states, ethnic groups, and regions that we now know as Yugoslavia. There is still a very strong and healthy woodwork tradition, however, utilizing all the old and ancient styles and forms. Many of the patterns, designs, and motifs are recognizably Christian, Turkish, and Roman; there is still a great affection for Roman eagles, Christian crosses, and Turkish pattern forms.

Apart from a limited amount of carving and painting on such basic items as beds, chairs, tables, and stools, the carved and painted folk art best finds expression on the house exteriors, on the large dower chests, and on the many small domestic wares. Most of the designs appear to be a mixture of shallow notch-cut or chip-carved patterns, worked in with traditional stylized symbolic motifs. For example, a box or a gate post might be covered with an overall design of chip-carved zigzags, gridded lines, cross-hatching, and space-filling chip-cut patterns. And within this design, there might also be Christian crosses, primitive pre-Christian severed heads, and coiled snakes. The folk carvers aren't necessarily aware that they are carving pre-Christian pagan motifs; they work the ancient patterns or motifs into the design simply because that's the way it has always been done.

The shepherd and peasant carvers take great pride in their carving skills and in the objects that they make and decorate. There are walking sticks and mugs, spoons and boxes, spindles and distaffs, all characteristically covered in stylized animal motifs and chip-carved patterns. As to the methodology, the wood is usually stained red, blue, or black, and then the patterns and motifs are knife-cut through the color to the white wood beneath. The designs and patterns are crisp, white, and sharp-edged, giving the appearance of being drawn and painted rather than incised.

Italy

Italy has seen many cultural comings and goings. It is an ancient country, a country with a uniquely rich folk art heritage.

4. Yugoslavia—detail from a whetstone holder; knife-worked, incised, and painted (nineteenth century).

5. Yugoslavia—a herdsman's beaker; knife-worked, carved in the round, incised, and pierced (nineteenth century).

6. Yugoslavia—detail from a distaff; knife-worked, chip-carved (nineteenth century).

4

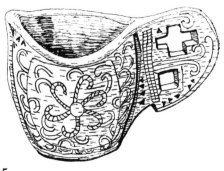

5

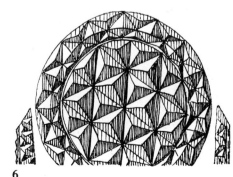

6

Geographically, Italy can be divided into three main regions: the northern mountains, or Alps; the central plains; and the southern Mediterranean coast. And, as you might expect, the climate and geography create a domino effect that shapes the folk art woodwork. The geography and the climate shape the people, the people and the geography shape the houses, leading to the factors that give shape to the folk art woodwork.

The northern Alpine houses are made of wood and designed to be warm, protective, and comfortable. The emphasis is on indoor comfort, and so there is a lot of heavy furniture. Three factors—the wood, the furniture, and the climatic necessity for indoor activities—shape the folk art environment. The furniture is richly and painstakingly carved, the wall panels are carved and painted, and generally everything is carefully and painstakingly decorated. The Alpine regions are particularly rich in folk art woodwork; there are huge wooden bedsteads, massive tables, benches, chairs, and chests, all richly embellished with patterns, designs, and motifs.

Down south, on the other hand, on the warm Mediterranean coast where the houses are made of stone and plaster, the folk art environment is quite different. Since people spend the greater part of the year out of doors, the emphasis is not on carved and decorated interiors and large pieces of furniture, but rather on small, portable, highly decorative personal articles.

The southern folk art woodworkers therefore favor small highly carved items: stools, cradles, small chairs, boxes, and all the usual items of kitchen and hall ware. The designs and patterns used are simple naïve forms. The southern Italian peasant style is characterized by small motifs—circles, zigzags, rosettes, crossed-hatched textures, and triangles—all variously painted, chip-carved, and incised.

Greece

Greek folk art woodwork has long drawn inspiration from both the East and the West—from Europe and from the Orient. This is not to say that the folk art has become blurred or is any way diminished, but rather that it is particularly rich in multicultural patterns and techniques. The Greek folk artists have, as it were, tasted foreign patterns and designs, and then they have absorbed them and unknowingly used them in their own art forms.

Greece is split geographically, and so there are many local styles and forms. This being so, it's not easy to put an overall name to the Greek folk art style. What one can say is that the village and peasant woodwork is characterized by its liveliness, its naïveté, and above all by its spontaneity. Geometrical patterns, circles, zigzags, curves, spirals, swastikas, and textural infills abound.

Within these traditional pattern forms or settings, there are a great many individual designs and motifs. So, for example, a wooden distaff might be gracefully curved, pierced, and patterned with spirals, edged with a chip-carved border, or there might be a series of chip-carved and incised roundels, or the areas around the roundels might be infilled with small chip-carved triangles. And then, finally, the folk artist might have worked in his own initials or a little personal scene drawn from his own everyday surroundings as a signature.

1. Italy—detail from a baker's stamp; knifeworked; carved in shallow relief so as to stamp/print a positive image (nineteenth century).

2. Greece—detail from a distaff; knifeworked, cut, pierced, and incised (nineteenth century).

3. Spain—detail from a chest; knife- and gouge-worked, carved in shallow relief, incised, and chip-carved (eighteenth century).

1

2

3

Western and Central Europe

Spain

In evaluating folk art woodwork, Spain has often been described as "the biggest, the best, and the most diverse." Of course it's not really possible to make such a sweeping judgment, and it's highly subjective to place countries in a sort of folk art "highest ratings" list. But if there *were* such a grading system, Spain would surely rank very high among those countries with a living and flourishing folk art tradition.

Spain is undoubtedly unique as far as folk art woodwork is concerned. This is true not only because of the huge variety of its woodwork, which is extremely varied and exciting, but also because the designs and patterns are a wonderful coming together of a great number of different cultural styles.

For hundreds of years, Spain has been the meeting place, or crossroads, for many cultures. Africa, the Arab world, Portugal, France, and the Americas—at one time or another, all these countries and cultures have, through trade, conquest, or colonization, greatly influenced Spain. Spanish folk art woodwork is unique in that it contains patterns and motifs from just about every corner of the globe. There are patterns from regions and cultures as far apart in time, space, and tradition as tribal black Africa, the Middle East, Iran, and Mexico.

Spain is also highly diverse in its many differing geographical and climatic zones. There are warm lush coasts and well-forested regions, barren deserts and rugged mountain ranges. Consequently, there is a tremendous variation in living conditions, which affects the many different styles, patterns, forms, and techniques of folk art woodwork.

The patterns and decorations of Spain's tables, chairs, chests, beds, cradles, and cupboards (many of them well carved and painted) have won universal praise. But best of all, we think, are the small, naïvely carved items that are still being made and used by shepherds, herdsmen, and peasants. Of all these many wonderfully exuberant items, the most exciting in terms of pattern are the distaffs, the shepherds' crooks, the love spoons, and the various stamps and presses that are used in the making of bread, pastry, and cheese.

The patterns and decorations are characterized by being knife-worked, incised, chip-carved, and sometimes painted or stained. Although in most regions the designs tend to be geometrical, occasionally the distaffs and love spoons are decorated with figurative carving and then further embellished with metal and bone inlay, as well as brass pins.

4. Spain—detail from a flax swingle; knife-worked, pierced, and shaped (nineteenth century).

5. Czechoslovakia—gingerbread mould; knife- and gouge-worked, carved in shallow relief so as to stamp a positive image (nineteenth century).

6. Czechoslovakia—gingerbread mould; knife- and gouge-worked, carved in shallow relief so as to stamp/print a positive image (nineteenth century).

4

5

6

Czechoslovakia

Czechoslovakia has a vigorous and vital folk art woodwork tradition. The focus of interest shifts, however, from region to region, from wooden houses with large pieces of furniture to small items of kitchen and hall ware. For example, on the relatively treeless plains, where the houses tend to be built of brick and stone, the emphasis is on small, highly decorative, portable personal items like, say, distaffs, spoons, and small pieces of furniture. But in the well-forested areas of Bohemia and Wallachia, as you would expect, just about everything is made of wood. The houses themselves are wood, the rooms within are panelled with generous timbers, and most of the rooms are well stocked with massive wooden furniture.

In northeast Bohemia, the wooden houses are of particular interest. The walls are built from cut-and-squared logs, the gable walls overhang the front door and are massively built from diagonally placed planks, and the whole structure is trimmed and decorated with pierced and carved scallop-edged boards. The interiors are just as generously timbered, decorated, and patterned. The panelled walls and the larger pieces of furniture are variously deep-gouge carved, painted, and incised with geometrical motifs, painted with flowers, and decorated with motifs or inlay.

Germany and Austria

Germany and Austria have an unusually diverse folk art woodwork tradition. Unusual for their versatility, folk art woodworkers have applied their skills to the making of everything from furniture, carved beams for houses, carved "horses' head" gable beams for roof tops, tower clocks, baskets, carts and boxes to pastry boards, sledges, love tokens, and, of course, toys.

While recognizing the magnificent items of German furniture—the chairs, beds, chests, bridle chairs, the washing and mangle boards, and all the rest—we feel the best of the artifacts, and certainly the most well known, are the small whittled, turned, carved, and painted working toys—the Arks and animals, the moving and swinging figures, and the little wheeled toys.

If you want to discover a uniquely exciting and interesting aspect of European folk art woodwork, you'll find none more intriguing than Austrian and German toys. Particularly noteworthy are the toys that were (and are) made in the Groden valley in the southern Austrian Tyrol, and those made in such German towns and districts as Thuringia, Nuremberg, Oberammergau, and Berchtesgaden.

1. Germany—rocking-horse toy; lathe-, saw-, knife-, and gouge-worked, turned, fitted, and painted (late nineteenth century).

2. Austria—gingerbread mould; knife- and gouge-worked, carved in shallow relief so as to stamp/print a positive image (eighteenth century).

3. Switzerland—milk pail detail; knife-worked, incised line (eighteenth century).

Switzerland

Although Switzerland has a wonderfully rich folk art woodwork tradition, it is difficult to define its qualities and idiosyncrasies. The sum total of Swiss folk art is a coming together of Austrian, German, Italian, and French traditions. In many ways, Swiss folk art woodwork displays the best characteristics of Austrian, German, Italian, and French folk art, plus those native qualities that make it typically Swiss. Of

1

2

3

course, depending on the region, the various folk art forms do appear to be Austrian, German, or whatever, but on closer scrutiny, there is an overall style that makes Swiss patterns, motifs, and forms quite distinctive.

Swiss folk art woodwork best finds expression in the houses, the toys, and all the smaller items of domestic ware. From valley to valley, many of the traditional houses have decorative timbers, fretted and pierced balconies, and carved doors. All the exterior woodwork is, to a greater or lesser degree, painted in large blocks of color, highlighted with colored patterns, and otherwise embellished with carved, fretted, and painted patterns and details.

Swiss folk art is famous for its carved and painted dower chests, its relief-carved beds, the carved, fretted, and painted cradles, as well as the decorated tables, cupboards, and all the rest. Nonetheless, we think that more than any other form, Swiss folk art woodwork is special for the quality of its small Alpine wares. The herdsmen and shepherds traditionally make the most beautiful toys, walking sticks, milking stools, love tokens, spinning distaffs, presses, bowls, dishes, and boxes. These are wonderfully and sensitively decorated with delicate incised and chip-carved patterns, designs, and motifs. The carvers and decorators favor such patterns and motifs as roundels, chip-carved triangles, scratch-carved tulips, and figurative designs taken from everyday life, with all the areas in and around the main designs infilled with all manner of line and cross-hatched textures.

4. England—Windsor chair splat designs; saw-worked, fretted, and pierced (eighteenth century).

5. England, Christchurch Priory, Hampshire —misericord seat detail; knife- and gouge-worked, carved in deep relief with undercuts (early sixteenth century).

6. England—busk detail; knife-worked, incised, and chip-carved (eighteenth century).

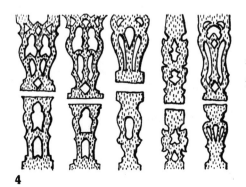

4

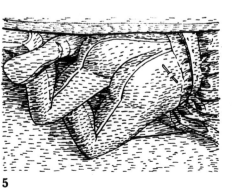

5

6

The British Isles

England

England has a long and glorious tradition of folk art woodwork, a tradition that encompasses a great variety of techniques, usages, and forms of decoration. These extend from medieval church carvings, domestic furniture, and kitchen and dairy wares to ships' figureheads, painted canal boats, and fairground carousel horses. However, the English tradition is, in part, made up of such diverse and apparently unrelated elements that it is better in many ways not to think of it as a unified whole. The various facets and forms of English folk art woodwork are best understood if they are considered individually.

Although, of course, at some time or other in the distant past, the tradition of fine style and fashion furniture did originate and flower from folk art woodwork, but from quite an early period a good deal of English furniture was made in large city workshops. With this transition, there evolved a style and standard that sets it outside what we now consider to be the folk art tradition. In discussing English furniture, the term "folk art furniture" is now understood primarily to mean individual, country-made, pre-eighteenth-century furniture. This includes the benches, chests, tables, dressers, beds, chests of drawers, and of course the particular type of composite bentwood, stick-back, adze-worked, slab-seated chair now known as a Windsor, or a country, chair.

English folk furniture tends to be restrained, with the pattern forms referring not so much to any applied decoration, but rather to the total shape and structure of the piece. Of course, some items are decorated; for example, many dressers have pierced fret-cut front boards, some early pieces have deep carving and pierced roundels, and some Windsor chairs have simple pierced and carved back-splat motifs. But, for the most part, folk furniture is undecorated.

It has been said that the English folk art furniture tradition reached its peak with medieval church furniture, that is, with bench ends and misericord seats. Such pieces, worked in oak, are wonderfully deep-gouge carved and undercut, with a great many naturalistic designs taken from everyday life. If your interest is in three-dimensional imagery—figures in costume, animals, and the like —rather than, say,

1. England—shop sign detail advertising cigar; knife- and gouge-worked, relief-carved (nineteenth century).

2. England—ship's figurehead; knife- and gouge-worked, carved in the round, and painted (eighteenth century).

3. England, Bristol—fairground galloper, carved by A. Anderson; knife- and gouge-worked, deep relief-carved, and painted (nineteenth century).

1

2

3

flat patterns or repeated geometrical motifs, then your focus should be on the medieval misericords of the oldest English minsters, priories, and cathedrals—Ely, Christchurch, Lincoln, and the others.

Among the small domestic items—the various presses, boards, bowls, and all the small personal dress and toiletry wares—our impression is that the carved corset rods, or busks, are the most fascinating. Busks were made to be slid down, as a kind of stiffening, into the front, or bodice, of a woman's dress. Decorated with all kinds of scratch-carved and chip-carved designs, patterns, and motifs, eighteenth-century busks are particularly interesting because these love token designs are often so personal. By their very nature, and because busks were so intimately hidden from view, many of the designs and patterns are remarkably uninhibited—usually the decorations include lovers' hearts, dates, and initials, and the little personal intimacies that might be exchanged between lovers.

Perhaps the most exciting, and certainly the largest examples, of English folk art woodwork are the ships' figureheads and the variety of fairground figures—the galloping horses and large carousel roosters. There is a historic linkup between the figureheads and the merry-go-round horses. When the ships' figurehead carvers were put out of business by the coming of steamships, the newly invented steam engines made possible the gigantic fairground carousels, which in turn gave rise to the craft of fairground horse and figure carving.

Fortunately for the former ships' figurehead carvers, when the ironclad ships made figureheads obsolete, they were able to slip out of one trade and into another almost without having to change the style or even the scale of their work. Both ships' figureheads and the fairground carvings are characterized by being built up, by being bolder and larger than life, by their deep-gouge carving, and by being painted and embellished with brilliant, bright primary colors with lots of gold leaf.

A singular expression of English folk art woodwork lies in the wonderfully painted, uniquely beautiful canal narrow boats. With the English canal system coming into being in the half century between, say, 1790 and 1840, and then continuing on until the late 1960s, "narrow," or "long," boats were once a familiar sight on most English inland waterways. These slender, brightly painted boats, used to transport such commodities as coal, iron, and pottery, were also home for countless families of boat people, or "water Romanies." In many ways these canal boat families were more like gypsies or fairground travellers, and as such, they were a floating population set apart from ordinary village and town folk.

The narrow boats play a special role in the history of English folk art, because they gave expression to a uniquely beautiful (if un-English) type of woodwork decoration. Interiors and exteriors were characteristically painted and decorated with a great variety of geometrical designs: playing card "hearts," "clubs," "diamonds," and "spades" motifs; naïve flower patterns; and stylized "rose and castle" pictures. As to the origins of canal boat art, it is thought that there is perhaps some sort of tie-in with the painterly arts of European gypsies, Czechoslovakian wagon painting, and the designs and motifs that were painted by the Pennsylvanian Germans. In point of fact, Dutch and German engineers and laborers were used to build the canals, and it is quite possible that they brought their folk art traditions with them.

4. England—canal boat painting; oil on wood, by Frank Nurser (early twentieth century).

5. Wales—love spoon; knife-worked, whittled, pierced, and chip-carved (nineteenth century).

6. Scotland—a quaich/drinking bowl detail, showing the "feathered" joints (nineteenth century).

4

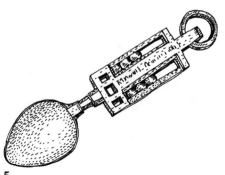

5

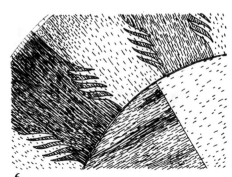

6

Scotland, Ireland, and Wales

With regard to folk art woodwork, Scotland, Ireland, and Wales are linked by at least four factors. All three countries were deforested by the middle of the eighteenth century; they all traditionally have rural economies; they were all remote, isolated, and poor; and, finally, all three were, to a greater or lesser extent, subjugated by the English and systematically depopulated by famine and enforced emigration. These historical misfortunes contributed to a diminished folk art woodwork tradition.

This is certainly not to say that the Scots, Welsh, or Irish were, or are, culturally impoverished. To the contrary, all three countries have wonderful folk traditions in literature, poetry, singing, music, dancing, and such. However, the poor, insecure living conditions never really encouraged the development of confident, settled folk art woodwork. Nevertheless, there is a tradition for making small portable domestic items—beautifully carved, pierced, and decorated love spoons; carved, plank-back spinning stools; and small bowls known as "coggies," or quaiches.

Love spoons are traditionally labors of love that were carved by lovers and presented to their sweethearts. Known to the British as Welsh love spoons, they are also extensively made and carved in Ireland and Scotland. They were (and are) usually more or less spoon-shaped and variously knife-worked, scratch-carved, pierced, and whittled with all kinds of small stylized and figurative patterns and motifs. The most popular designs are entwined love hearts, compass-worked hex circles, and little collections of caged balls. The balls symbolize togetherness, as well as the desired number of children.

It is thought that love spoons got their name from the old English term "to spoon," meaning "to kiss and cuddle," or even from the earlier Anglo-Saxon word "spon," meaning "to chip or splinter." Whatever the case, love spoons are by their very nature extravagant, individual, and exuberant expressions of skill.

There is also in Scotland a tradition for making a curious four-legged, plank-back type of chair, or stool. Known as Orkney spinning stools, or even as Gaelic spinning chairs, these naïve, basic types of stick-legged seats belong to the archetypal country cottage-chair tradition. Such chairs usually have a slab seat, four knife-carved or turned stick legs, and a relief-carved plank back. The designs usually include national symbols like roses and thistles, and entwined Gaelic running patterns.

Quaiches, caups, cogues, or even "cuach"—from the Gaelic meaning "dish" or "cup"—are curious stave-built bowls. Traditionally made in Scotland, they are built in a barrel-like manner of alternate staves of contrasting wood. Technically these bowls are quite sophisticated. The staves are locked together by a series of edge-to-edge feather cuts and then strapped with hoops of willow wood. Resplendent in their simple naïveté, these bowls are, as far as we know, unique to the Gaelic folk art woodwork tradition.

1. America—dower chest detail; painted (nineteenth century).

2. America—rocking-chair detail; gold-on-black stencil (nineteenth century).

3. America—Mahantango Valley, Pa. miniature dough trough, painted (nineteenth century).

1

2

3

America

Introduction

The United States has a uniquely diverse tradition of folk art woodwork, a tradition that is therefore wonderfully rich and varied. This grows out of the fact that America represents a coming together of many separate traditions. In its infancy the New World was populated by Europeans, that is, by immigrants and refugees who by the very nature of the circumstances of their lives yearned after the aura of "the old country." And so there developed an idealized image or notion of what it had been like "back home."

In this highly charged emotional atmosphere, the new Americans went out of their way to nurture and nourish all the folk arts and crafts that reminded them of the mother country. When, for example, a Polish settler set out to make a chest or a toy, he didn't necessarily consciously decide to make it in the Polish tradition. He simply did what he had always done, making one in the tradition he had absorbed back home. Consequently, because the woodworkers were working from memory, and because they were using pioneer tools, techniques, and materials, and because some of them were simply untrained, the new folk art woodwork developed a curious out-of-focus, naïve, larger-than-life quality that we now think of as being characteristically American.

Typically, and certainly compared to the European folk art of the same period, colors are bolder, forms are more primitive, patterns are exaggerated, and designs are uninhibited and used in different ways. It has been said that American folk art woodwork is a gloriously unrestrained mishmash of all the best of the Old World —with an exhilarating touch of the New.

Furniture

American folk art furniture is a wonderful blending of Old-World designs, patterns, motifs, folk customs, and traditional techniques and New World pioneer make-do-and-mend know-how. In the pioneer/settler setting, patterns were borrowed from neighboring communities, native woods were disguised under layers of paint, and furniture was decorated in a variety of ways. It was handpainted with garlands of flowers, stencilled, geometrically patterned, carved, textured, gilded, varnished, combed,

4. America—wall panel detail; stencil-printed (nineteenth century).

5. America, Mass.—floor detail; stencil-printed, and varnished (eighteenth century).

6. America—merganser decoy; knife-worked, carved in the round, and painted (nineteenth century).

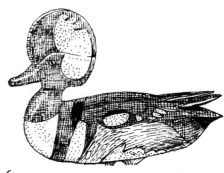

4

5

6

and grained until it became, unwittingly, a uniquely beautiful pastiche, a half-remembered echo of Old-World types and styles. In this wonderfully enriched folk art environment, images, forms, and patterns were freely adapted, and all kinds of furniture were made and decorated in an exciting, new, and uninhibited way, a way that we now consider to be characteristically American.

Stencilling

When the European settlers left their homelands to build new lives in the American wilderness, they couldn't afford imported luxuries, like carpets, wallpaper, and pictures. However, spurred on by the need for color and pattern, the settlers quickly developed their own decorative crafts, and stencilling was one of them. Drawing inspiration from their various mother-country traditions—German *fractur* painting, Swedish rosemaling, and others—the new Americans decorated their walls, floors, and furniture with all kinds of stencilled friezes, patterns, and pictures.

Soon itinerant stencillers and painters were travelling around the countryside, decorating to order. Working with very basic materials, like oiled cards, homemade brushes, and paints made from earth colors and milk, the stencillers were soon decorating walls, floors, and furniture with strikingly characteristic crisp-edged designs and patterns. Caught up in the zeitgeist, they favored strong, bold designs, like leaf-and-flower borders, flowers, trees, bells, eagles, and doves.

Decoys

Duck decoys are simply imitation ducks that were originally used to lure wild fowl into gun traps. The word "decoy" comes from the Dutch words *kooj* and *koye*, meaning "to lure, entice, and snare." The remarkable thing is that traditional American folk art duck decoys were whittled, carved, and painted by just about everybody and anybody. If a settler wanted to go duck shooting, or if he lived near water and just liked whittling, then as like as not he would spend a good deal of his spare time making decoys. And, of course, the decoys were made to resemble all kinds of bird life—everything from geese, swans, and snipes to herons, loons, and mergansers.

Duck decoys are made from wood, and can be carved realistically or as abstract bird forms. They can be gouged or hatchet- or rasp-worked, and can be painted or left unpainted.

1. America—hobby horse; sawn and gouge-worked, built-up, carved, and jointed (nineteenth century).

2. America, Rhode Island—stern board detail; knife- and gouge-worked, built-up, carved in the round, and painted (nineteenth century).

3. America—tavern sign; painted (nineteenth century).

Toys

Traditional American folk art woodwork toys are quite beautiful and varied. There are painted and stencil-decorated Arks complete with Mr. and Mrs. Noah and multiple rows of animals. There are dolls and soldiers, hobbyhorses and farm animals, bats and balls, and all kinds of working toys that click, move, and spin.

1

2

3

In times past, if a child wanted a pull-along horse or whatever, then one of his parents would make one, or they would have one made to order by the local carver, whittler, joiner, or shipcarver. And, of course, as these folk art toymakers drew their inspiration from European models as well as from their surroundings, so the toys are, at one and the same time, bold, traditional, sturdy, well-made, and naïve. Today these toys have a special age-old quality that is probably an unconscious mixture of Old-World realism and New World abstraction.

Figureheads and Shop Signs

As the American economy developed, so shipping became more and more important, with shipyards and shipcarvers setting up business all along the Eastern Seaboard. The carving workshops were busy places, with the master carvers and their apprentices working on just about everything from massive, nine-foot-high, head-and-shoulder figures to various small, relief-carved stern boards. When business was slack, the carvers would supplement their regular pay by carving less prestigious works. Consequently, it was quite common for these carvers to work on shop signs, portraits, cigar-store figures, and toys.

Characteristically, American figureheads were made of easy-to-carve pine. They were carved and painted in such a way that they could best be seen in profile—the lines and colors being bold, brilliant, vigorous, and uncomplicated.

Weather Vanes and Whirligigs

In the context of this book, weather vanes and whirligigs are considered to be woodworked, wind-driven sculptures.

Weather vanes are carved, painted, and pivoted "wind flags" that swing around in the wind. Early American carvers favored strong flat shapes and simple bold designs—such as horses, Indians, and roosters—that could be seen and instantly recognized at a distance silhouetted against the sky.

Whirligigs are a delightful mixture of weather vane and windmill. Made of wood and variously carved, turned, painted, pivoted, and crank-operated, these puppetlike figures—usually soldiers, Indians with paddles, or figures on bicycles—are automatons that draw their power from the wind.

4. America—Noah's Ark toy; saw-, knife-, and gouge-worked, cut, carved, and painted (nineteenth century).

5. America—Indian weather vane; saw- and knife-worked, fretted, and painted (nineteenth century).

6. America—whirligig; fretted, and painted (nineteenth century).

4

5

6

Chapter One

Lines

Chip-Carved and Scratched

1. Switzerland—box design detail; knife-worked, chip-carved (nineteenth century).

2. Yugoslavia—distaff; knife-worked, chip-carved, pierced, and scratch-carved (nineteenth century).

3. Norway—detail from a kitchen board; knife-worked, chip-carved (nineteenth century).

4. Yugoslavia—detail from a distaff; knife-carved, pierced, chip-carved, and scratched (nineteenth century).

5. Norway—box lid detail; knife-worked, scratch-carved, and chip-carved (nineteenth century).

6. Norway—box lid detail; knife-worked, scratch-carved, and chip-carved (nineteenth century).

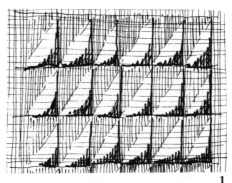

1

3

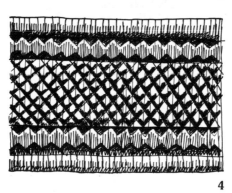

4

5

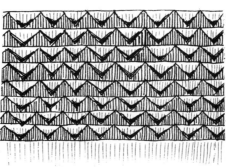

6

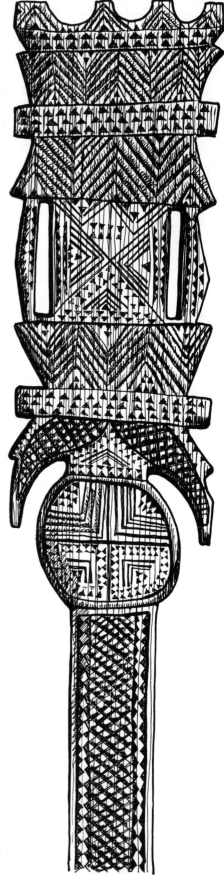

2

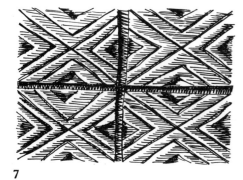

7

9

10

11

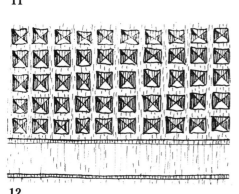

12

8

7. Yugoslavia, Dalmatia—detail from a distaff; knife-carved, pierced, chip-carved, and scratched (nineteenth century).

8. Yugoslavia, Dalmatia—top half of a distaff; knife-carved, pierced, scratched, and chip-carved (nineteenth century).

9. Sweden—detail from a box; painted and knife-worked, chip-carved, and scratched (nineteenth century).

10. Yugoslavia, Dalmatia—detail from a distaff; knife-worked, incised, and chip-carved (nineteenth century).

11. Yugoslavia—detail from a distaff; knife-worked, painted, and chip-carved (nineteenth century).

12. Norway—box side detail; knife-worked, chip-carved, and incised (nineteenth century).

Swedish Curves and Zigzags

1. Sweden—detail from a distaff; knife-worked, scratch-carved, and chip-carved (nineteenth century).

2. Sweden—detail from a watch stand; knife-carved, pierced, gouge-carved, and painted (early nineteenth century).

3. Sweden—detail from a weaving tool; knife-worked, pierced, and painted (nineteenth century).

4. Sweden—detail from a weaving knife; knife-worked, chip-carved, and scratched (nineteenth century).

5. Sweden—detail from a distaff; knife-worked, pierced, painted, and chip-carved (nineteenth century).

6. Sweden—detail from a porringer; knife-worked, drilled, and incised (nineteenth century).

7. Sweden—detail from a bowl; knife-worked, gouge-worked, painted, and incised (eighteenth century).

8. Sweden—detail from a beer can; knife-worked, gouge-worked, chip-carved, and incised (eighteenth century?).

9. Sweden—detail from a bedpost; worked with knife and gouge, chip-carved, and incised (eighteenth century).

10. Sweden—detail from a porringer; worked with a gouge and knife, incised, and drilled (nineteenth century).

1

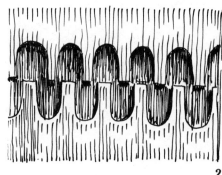

2

3

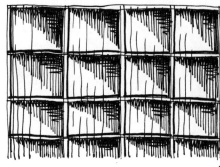

4

5

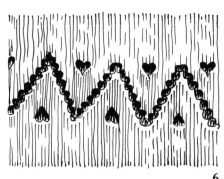

6

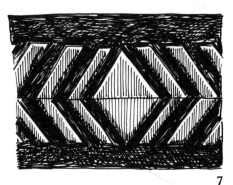

7

8

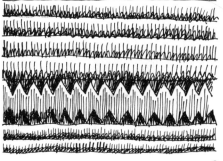

9

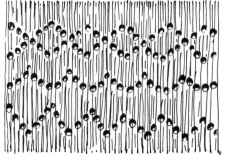

10

11

12

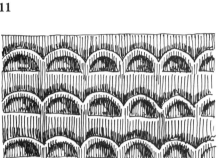

13

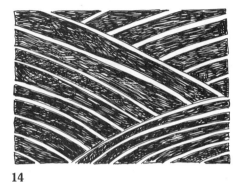

14

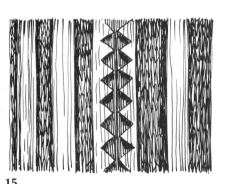

15

16

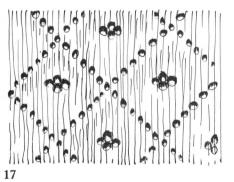

17

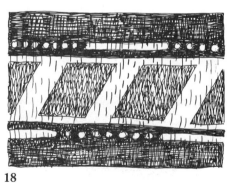

18

19

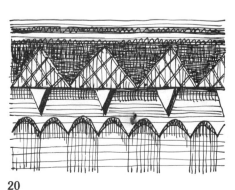

20

11. Sweden—detail from a door handle; knife-worked, chip-carved, and incised (eighteenth century).

12. Sweden—detail from a distaff; knife-worked, pierced, painted, and scratch-carved (nineteenth century).

13. Sweden—detail from a beer stoop; gouge- and knife-worked (nineteenth century).

14. Sweden—detail from a weaving stick/tool; knife-worked, painted, and incised (nineteenth century).

15. Sweden—detail from a beer stoop; knife-whittled, incised, and chip-carved (nineteenth century).

16. Sweden—detail from a door handle; knife-worked, whittled, and incised (eighteenth century).

17. Sweden—detail from a beer stoop; knife-worked and drill-patterned (nineteenth century).

18. Sweden—detail from a beer can; knife- and gouge-worked, painted, and incised (nineteenth century).

19. Sweden—detail from a candlestick; knife-worked, painted, and incised (eighteenth century).

20. Sweden—detail from a porringer; knife- and gouge-worked, painted, relief-carved, and incised (nineteenth century).

33

Zigs and Zags

1. Hungary—detail from a weaver's shuttle; knife-worked, knife-incised, and drill-patterned (late nineteenth century).

2. Sweden—detail from a porringer; knife- and gouge-worked, poker-worked design (nineteenth century).

3. Sweden—detail from a beer can; worked with knife and drill, incised, and drill-patterned (early eighteenth century).

4. Yugoslavia—detail from a distaff; knife-worked, chip-carved, and incised (nineteenth century).

5. Norway—detail from a domestic bowl; knife-worked, incised, and scratched (eighteenth century).

6. Yugoslavia—detail from a whetstone holder; knife-worked, relief-carved, and incised (nineteenth century).

7. Poland—detail from a spoon rack; knife- and gouge-worked, pierced, and chip-carved (nineteenth century).

8. Sweden—detail from a distaff; knife-worked, relief-carved, chip-carved, and painted (nineteenth century).

9. France—detail from a weaver's headle/ tool; knife-worked, deeply chip-carved (early nineteenth century).

10. Sweden—detail from a distaff; knife-worked, relief-carved, incised, and chip-carved (early nineteenth century).

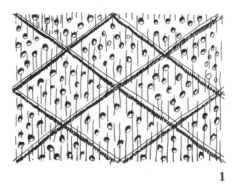

1

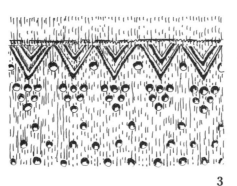

2

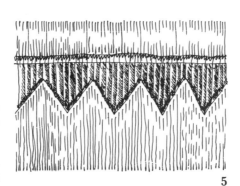

3

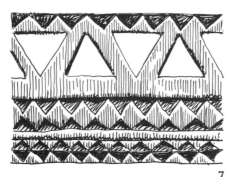

4

5

6

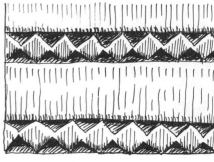

7

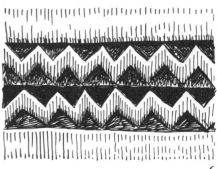

8

9

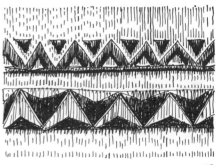

10

11

12

13

14

15

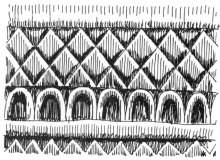

16

17

18

19

20

11. Sweden—detail from a spinning tool; knife-worked, pierced, incised, and painted (early nineteenth century).

12. Austria—detail from a washing beater; knife-worked, relief-carved, chip-carved, and incised (late nineteenth century).

13. France—detail from a weaver's headle; knife-worked, pierced, and incised (late eighteenth century).

14. Yugoslavia—detail from a whetstone holder; knife-worked, chip-carved, and stained (nineteenth century).

15. Romania—detail from a plaque; knife- and gouge-worked, relief-carved, and painted (early twentieth century).

16. Sweden—detail from a piece of harness/saddle; knife- and gouge-worked, relief-carved, incised, and chip-carved (nineteenth century).

17. Sweden—detail from a box; knife-worked, incised, relief-carved, and painted (eighteenth century).

18. Sweden—detail from a watch stand; knife- and gouge-worked, chip-carved, incised, and painted (nineteenth century).

19. Yugoslavia—detail from a whetstone box; knife-worked, incised, chip-carved, and stained (nineteenth century).

20. Yugoslavia—detail from a whetstone holder; knife-worked, chip-carved, incised, and stained (nineteenth century).

35

Marquetry and Inlay Checks

1. England(?)—detail from a "Nonesuch" chest; sawn thick block inlay (sixteenth century).

2. England(?)—detail from a "Nonesuch" chest; sawn thick block inlay (sixteenth century).

3. England(?)—detail from a "Nonesuch" chest; sawn thick block inlay (sixteenth century).

4. England—box detail; thin inlay (sixteenth century).

5. England—detail from a Tunbridgeware box; knife- and saw-worked, minute mosaic marquetry (nineteenth century).

1

2

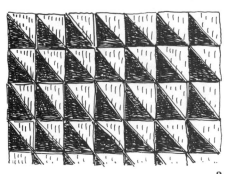

3

4

5

6. England(?)—detail from a "Nonesuch" desk; sawn thick block inlay (sixteenth century).

7. England(?)—detail from a "Nonesuch" chest; sawn thick block inlay (sixteenth century).

8. England(?)—detail from a "Nonesuch" chest; sawn thick block inlay (sixteenth century).

9. England(?)—detail from a "Nonesuch" chest; sawn thick block inlay (sixteenth century).

10. England(?)—detail from a "Nonesuch" desk; sawn thick block inlay (sixteenth century).

11. England(?)—detail from a "Nonesuch" box/chest; sawn thick block inlay (sixteenth century).

12. England(?)—detail from a "Nonesuch" box; sawn thick block inlay (sixteenth century).

13. England(?)—detail from a "Nonesuch" box; sawn thick block inlay (sixteenth century).

14. England(?)—detail from a "Nonesuch" chest/box; sawn thick block inlay (sixteenth century).

15. England(?)—detail from a "Nonesuch" chest/box; sawn thick block inlay (sixteenth century).

Painted and Stencilled

1. America—detail from a box; painted and stencil-decorated (nineteenth century).

2. England—detail from a box; painted and stencil-decorated border (nineteenth century).

3. America—detail from a piece of furniture; painted and stencil-decorated border (nineteenth century).

4. England—detail from a box; painted and stencil-decorated (nineteenth century).

5. America—detail from a floor design; painted, stencil-decorated, and varnished (nineteenth century).

6. England—detail from a box; painted and stencil-decorated (early twentieth century).

7. America—detail from a floor design; painted, stencil-decorated, and varnished (nineteenth century).

8. America—detail from a box; painted and stencil-decorated (nineteenth century).

9. America—detail from a floor design; painted, stencil-decorated, and varnished (nineteenth century).

10. America—detail from a floor design; painted, stencil-decorated, and varnished (nineteenth century).

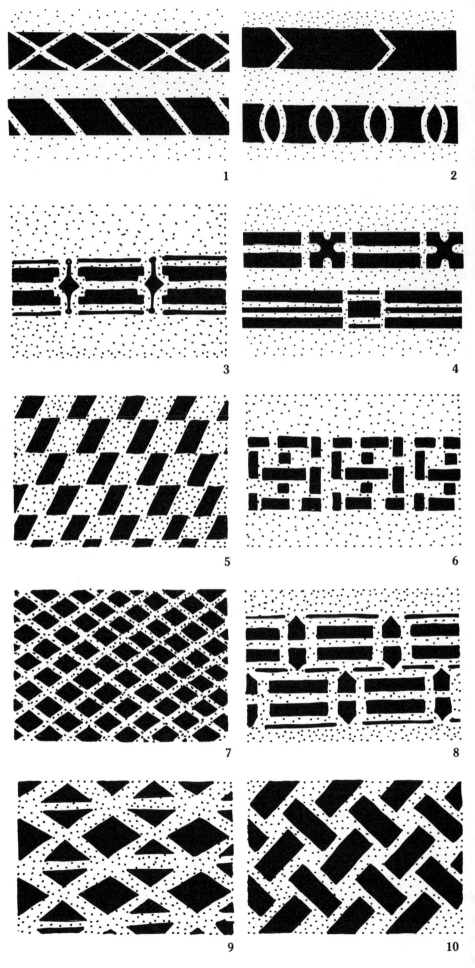

11

12

13

14

11. America—detail from a dower chest; painted (eighteenth century).

12. America—detail from a dower chest; painted (eighteenth century).

13. Russia—detail from a distaff; painted (nineteenth century).

14. Russia—detail from a distaff; painted (nineteenth century).

15. Russia—detail from a distaff; painted (nineteenth century).

15

39

Scandinavian Chip-Carved

1. Poland—detail from a spoon rack; knife-worked, chip-carved, pierced, and incised (mid-nineteenth century).

2. Norway—an armchair; lathe- and knife-worked, turned, carved, and chip-carved (fifteenth century).

1

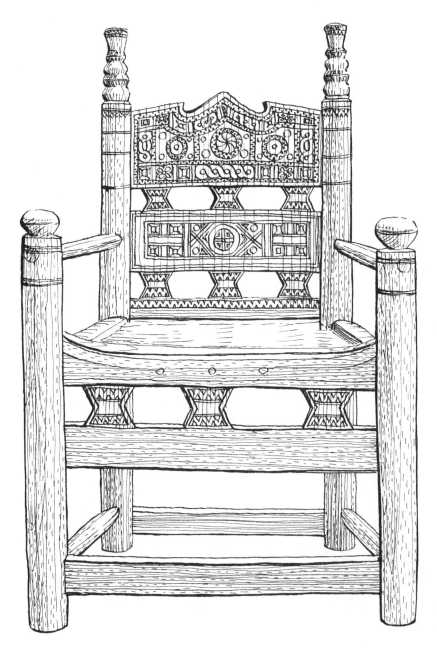

2

3

4

5

3. Latvia—detail from a distaff; knife-worked, carved, pierced, and chip-carved (mid-nineteenth century).

4. Yugoslavia—detail from a whetstone holder; knife-worked, chip-carved, and incised (nineteenth century).

5. France—detail from a weaving headle; knife-worked, pierced, and deeply chip-carved (late eighteenth century).

Spindles and Posts

1. Iceland—a winding pin; knife-worked, whittle-turned from one piece of wood, carved, incised, and chip-carved (eighteenth century?).

2. England—staircase spindles; lathe-turned (nineteenth century).

3. England—staircase spindles; lathe-turned (nineteenth century).

1

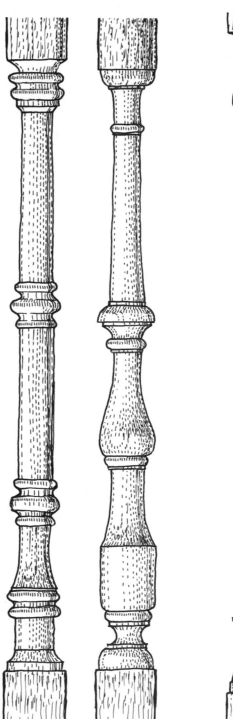

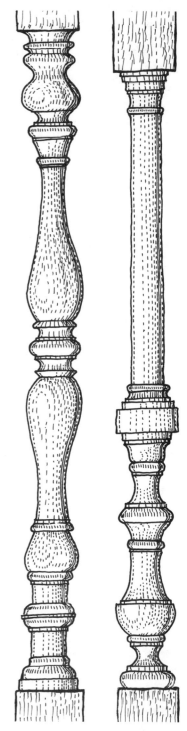

2

3

4

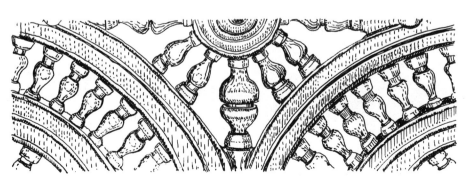

5

4. America, New England—a child's Windsor high chair; lathe-turned, adze-worked seat and steam-bent back (eighteenth century).

5. France—detail from a bedstead panel; carved, lathe-turned, and inlay mastic (late eighteenth century).

Stained, Painted, and Scratched

1. Sweden—detail from a bowl; gouge- and knife-worked, painted, and scratch-carved (early nineteenth century).

2. Sweden—detail from a bowl; worked with knife and gouge, painted, and scratch-carved (early nineteenth century).

3. Sweden—detail from a weaving tool; knife-worked, stained/painted, and scratch-carved (eighteenth century).

4. Romania—detail from a chest; gouge- and knife-worked, painted, and scratch-carved (eighteenth century).

5. Sweden—detail from a weaving stick/rod; worked with knife and gouge, stained, and scratch-carved (eighteenth century).

6. Romania—detail from a chest; worked with gouge and knife, painted, and scratch-carved (eighteenth century).

1

2

3

4

5

6

7

8

9

10

7. Hungary—detail from a chest; knife- and gouge-worked, painted, and scratch-carved (eighteenth century).

8. Hungary—detail from a chest; knife- and gouge-worked, painted, and scratch-carved (eighteenth century).

9. America—detail from a chest; knife- and gouge-worked, painted, and scratch-carved (seventeenth century).

10. Romania—detail from a chest; knife- and gouge-worked, painted, and scratch-carved (eighteenth century).

Pierced Hearts

1. Sweden—detail from a distaff; knife-worked, carved, pierced, and chip-carved (nineteenth century).

2. Sweden—house fence; sawn, fretted, and painted (early nineteenth century).

1

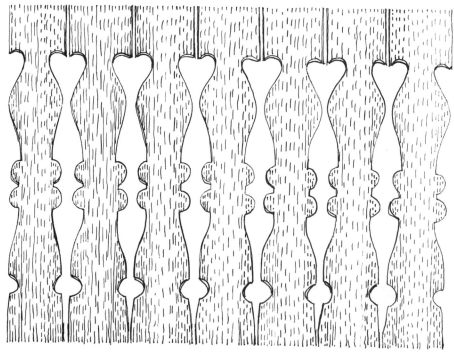

2

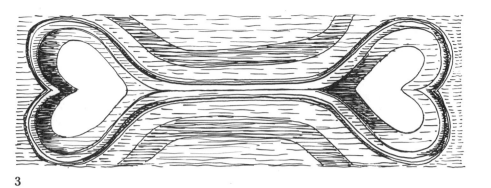

3

4

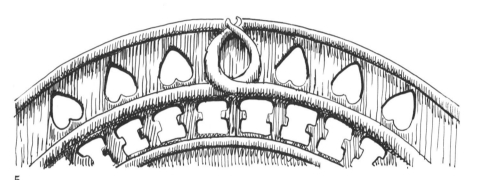

5

6

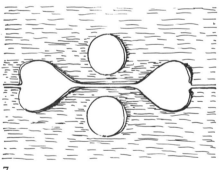

7

8

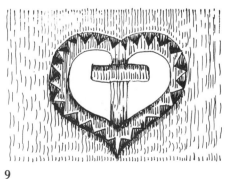

9

3. Sweden—detail from a distaff; knife- and gouge-worked, pierced, carved, and painted (early nineteenth century).

4. Sweden—detail from a distaff; sawn and knife-worked, pierced, and painted (nineteenth century).

5. Sweden—detail from a saddle; knife- and gouge-worked, sawn, carved, pierced, and painted (early nineteenth century).

6. Sweden—detail from a chair; sawn and knife-worked, pierced, and painted (early nineteenth century).

7. Sweden—detail from a hanging shelf; sawn and knife-worked, pierced, and painted (late eighteenth century).

8. Sweden—detail from a distaff; knife-worked, painted, pierced, chip-carved, and scratched (late nineteenth century).

9. Sweden—detail from a spoon; knife-worked, carved, pierced, and chip-carved (mid-nineteenth century).

Love Hearts

1. Wales—detail from a love spoon; whittled, pierced, and chip-carved (early nineteenth century).

2. Wales—detail from a love spoon; whittled, carved, pierced, and chip-carved (early nineteenth century).

3. Wales—detail from a love spoon; whittled, pierced, carved, and chip-carved (late eighteenth century).

4. Wales—detail from a love spoon; whittled, pierced, and carved (late eighteenth century).

5. Wales—detail from a love spoon; whittled and sawn, carved, and pierced (late eighteenth century).

1

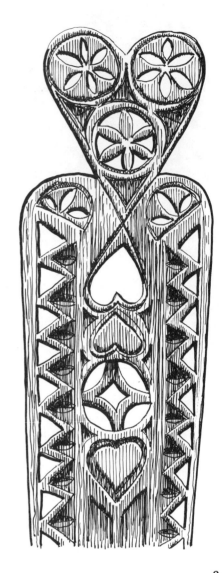

2

3

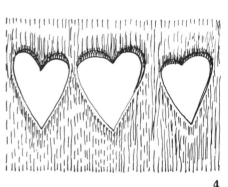

4

5

7

6

8

9

6. Austria—detail from a love token washing beater; knife-worked, chip-carved, incised, and stained (early nineteenth century).

7. Germany—detail from a yoke; knife- and gouge-worked, chip-carved, and incised (mid-nineteenth century).

8. Sweden—detail from a butter press; gouge- and knife-worked, relief-carved, and incised (mid-nineteenth century).

9. Wales—detail from a love spoon; knife-worked, shaped, pierced, and chip-carved (early nineteenth century).

49

American Stencils

1. America—furniture border detail; painted and stencilled (nineteenth century).

2. America—furniture border detail; painted and stencilled (nineteenth century).

3. America—chair decoration detail; painted and stencilled (nineteenth century).

4. America—chair decoration detail; painted and stencilled (nineteenth century).

5. America—furniture border detail; painted and stencilled (nineteenth century).

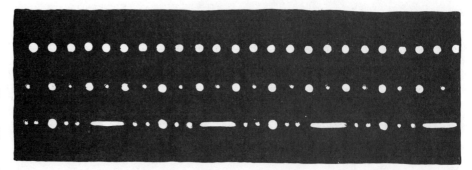

1

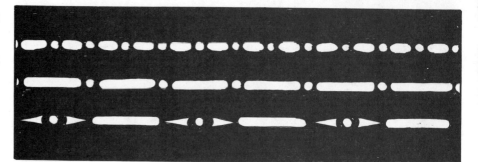

2

3

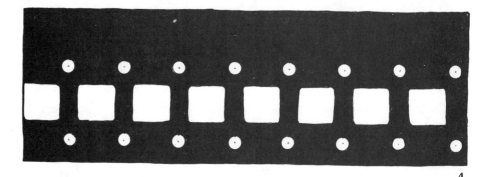

4

5

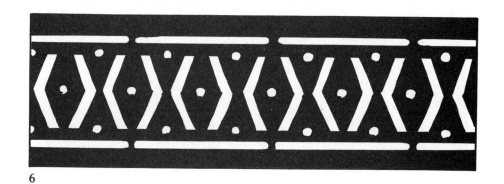

6

7

8

9

10

6. America—chair decoration detail; painted and stencilled (nineteenth century).

7. America—detail from a decorated "basket" chair; painted and stencilled (nineteenth century).

8. America—furniture border detail; painted and stencilled (early nineteenth century).

9. America—furniture border detail; painted and stencilled (nineteenth century).

10. America—detail from a gold-on-black furniture detail; painted, stencilled with bronze powder, and varnished (nineteenth century).

Welsh Love Spoons

1. Wales—love spoon; knife-worked, carved, pierced, whittled, relief-carved, and chip-carved (nineteenth century).

2. Wales—love spoon with "trapped ball"; knife-worked, carved, pierced, whittled, relief-carved, and chip-carved (nineteenth century).

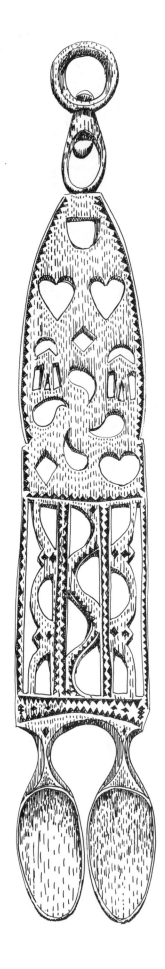

1

2

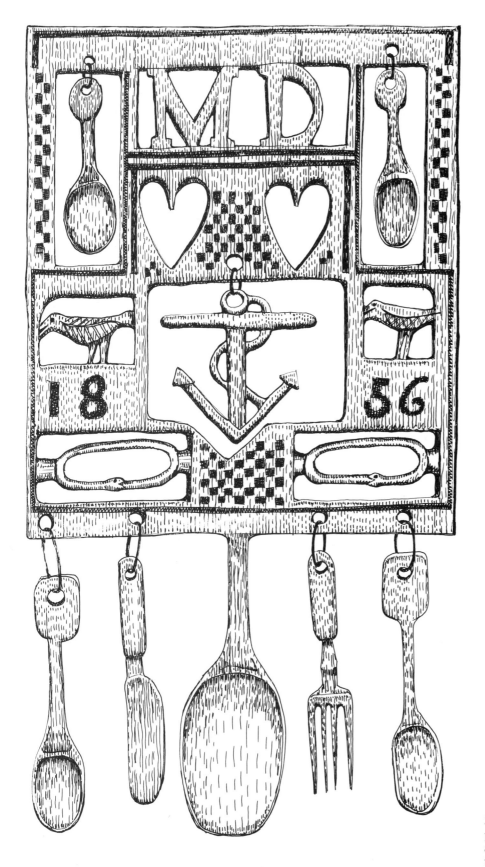

3. Wales—love spoon; knife-worked, carved, pierced, whittled, relief-carved, chip-carved, and mastic/wax inlaid (mid-nineteenth century).

3

Slab-Backs and Peg-Legs

1. Germany—a slab-back, peg-leg chair; saw-, gouge-, and knife-worked, fretted, pierced, jointed, and carved (mid-nineteenth century).

2. Poland—a slab-back chair detail; saw- and gouge-worked, pierced, and carved (early nineteenth century).

3. Poland—a slab-back chair detail; saw-, knife-, and gouge-worked, pierced, jointed, and carved (early nineteenth century).

4. Poland—a slab-back chair detail; saw-, knife-, drill-, and gouge-worked, pierced, and carved (early nineteenth century).

5. Romania—two slab-backs; knife-, saw-, and gouge-worked, sawn, pierced, and carved (nineteenth century).

6. Sweden—two slab-backs; knife-, saw-, and gouge-worked, sawn, pierced, and carved (nineteenth century).

1

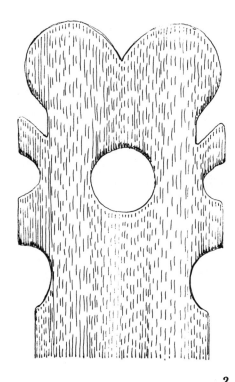

2

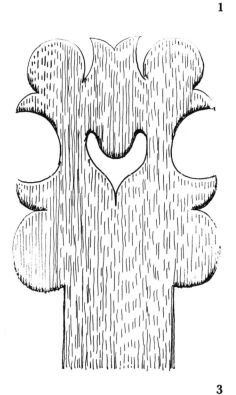

3

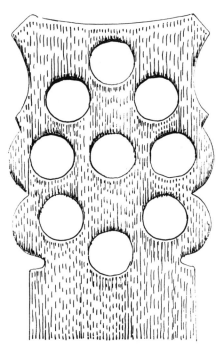

4

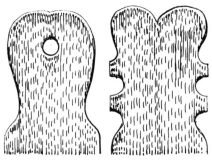

5

6

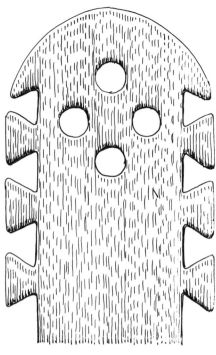

7

8

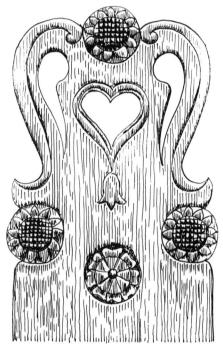

9

10

7. Romania—a slab-back chair detail; saw-, drill-, and gouge-worked, sawn, drilled, and carved (early nineteenth century).

8. Germany—a slab-back chair detail; saw-, drill-, and gouge-worked, sawn, drilled, and carved (early nineteenth century).

9. France—a slab-back chair detail; saw-, drill-, knife-, and gouge-worked, sawn, pierced, and carved (late eighteenth century).

10. Austria—a slab-back chair detail; saw-, drill-, gouge-, and knife-worked, sawn, pierced, carved, and relief-carved (early nineteenth century).

11. Romania—two slab-backs; saw-, drill-, and gouge-worked, sawn, pierced, and carved (nineteenth century).

12. Poland—two slab-backs; saw-, drill-, and gouge-worked, sawn, pierced, and carved (nineteenth century).

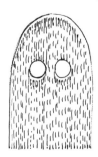

11

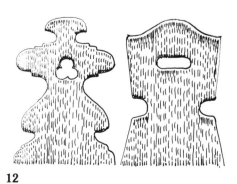

12

"Nonesuch" Inlay

1. England(?)—detail from a "Nonesuch" chest; saw and gouge work, sawn thick block inlay (late sixteenth century).

2. England(?)—detail from a "Nonesuch" chest; saw and gouge work, sawn thick block inlay (late sixteenth century).

1

2

3. England(?)—panel from a "Nonesuch" chest; saw and gouge work, sawn thick block inlay (sixteenth century).

3

Chapter Two

Circles

Swedish Circles

1. Sweden—birch-bark cigar case lid; hammer- and punch-worked, pressed, and incised (nineteenth century).

2. Sweden—detail from a distaff; knife-worked, whittled, pierced, and painted (nineteenth century).

3. Sweden—detail from a bedstead; knife- and gouge-worked, carved, and incised (eighteenth century).

4. Sweden—box detail; knife- and gouge-worked, relief-carved, and whittled (seventeenth century).

5. Sweden—detail from a large cupboard; knife- and gouge-worked, relief-carved, and whittled (eighteenth century).

1

2

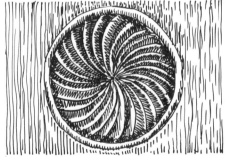

3

4

5

60

6

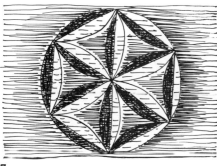

7

8

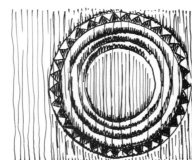

9

10

6. Sweden—detail from a bedpost; knife-and gouge-worked, relief-carved, and chip-carved (eighteenth century).

7. Sweden—detail from a bedstead; knife-and gouge-worked, carved, and chip-carved (eighteenth century).

8. Sweden—detail from a cigar case; hammer-, knife-, and punch-worked, pressed, and incised (nineteenth century).

9. Sweden—detail from a cigar case; hammer-, knife-, and punch-worked, pressed, and incised (nineteenth century).

10. Sweden—detail from a cigar case; hammer-, knife-, and punch-worked, pressed, and incised (nineteenth century).

Icelandic Circles

1. Iceland—box lid; knife- and gouge-worked, relief-carved, and incised (eighteenth century).

2. Iceland—detail from a hand mangle/beater; knife- and gouge-worked, relief-carved, and chip-carved (nineteenth century).

3. Iceland—detail from a hand mangle/beater; knife- and gouge-worked, relief-carved, and chip-carved (nineteenth century).

4. Iceland—detail from a bed board; gouge- and knife-worked, relief-carved, and incised (eighteenth century).

5. Iceland—detail from a bed board; gouge- and knife-worked, relief-carved, and incised (nineteenth century).

1

2

3

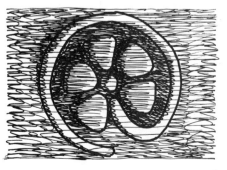

4

5

6

7

8

9

10

6. Iceland—box lid detail; gouge- and knife-worked, relief-carved, and incised (nineteenth century).

7. Iceland—box lid detail; gouge- and knife-worked, relief-carved, incised, and chip-carved (eighteenth century).

8. Iceland—detail from a knitting needle case; knife-worked, relief-carved, and incised (nineteenth century).

9. Iceland—detail from a bed board; gouge- and knife-worked, relief-carved, incised, and chip-carved (nineteenth century).

10. Iceland—box lid; gouge- and knife-worked, relief-carved, chip-carved, and incised (eighteenth century).

Swedish Circles

1. Sweden—detail from a watch stand; knife- and gouge-worked, carved, whittled, chip-carved, and incised (eighteenth century).

2. Sweden—detail from a distaff; knife-worked, whittled, and chip-carved (eighteenth century).

3. Sweden—detail from a hand mangle/beater; knife-worked, chip-carved, and incised (nineteenth century).

4. Sweden—detail from a hand mangle/beater; knife-worked, chip-carved, and incised (nineteenth century).

5. Sweden—detail from a hand mangle/beater; knife-worked, incised, and chip-carved (nineteenth century).

1

2

3

4

5

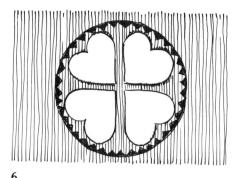

6

7

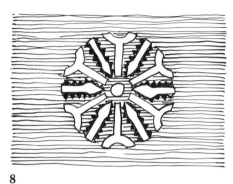

8

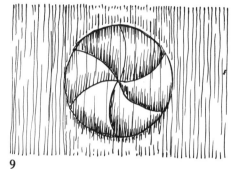

9

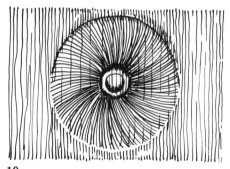

10

11

12

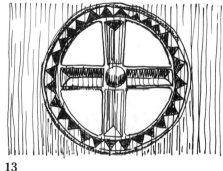

13

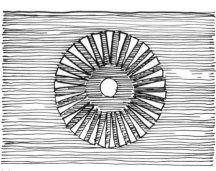

14

15

6. Sweden—detail from a distaff; knife-worked, whittled, pierced, painted, and chip-carved (nineteenth century).

7. Sweden—detail from a washing bat; knife-worked, relief-carved, and incised (nineteenth century).

8. Sweden—detail from a distaff; knife-worked, pierced, carved, painted, and chip-carved (nineteenth century).

9. Sweden—detail from a distaff; knife-worked, shallow relief-worked, and painted (nineteenth century).

10. Sweden—detail from a distaff; knife-worked, shallow relief-carved, incised, and painted (nineteenth century).

11. Sweden—detail from a hand mangle/beater; knife-worked, relief-carved, and incised (nineteenth century).

12. Sweden—detail from a distaff; knife-worked, carved, pierced, chip-carved, and painted (nineteenth century).

13. Sweden—detail from a hand mangle/beater; knife worked, relief carved, pierced, and chip-carved (nineteenth century).

14. Sweden—detail from a distaff; knife-worked, pierced, carved, and painted (nineteenth century).

15. Sweden—detail from a hand mangle/beater; knife-worked, whittled, relief-carved, and chip-carved (nineteenth century).

Chip-Carved Circles

1. Norway—bed end detail; saw-, knife-, and gouge-worked, sawn, carved, relief-carved, chip-carved, and incised (seventeenth century?).

2. England—panel detail; gouge- and knife-worked, relief-carved, and chip-carved (nineteenth century).

3. Sweden—hand mangle/beater detail; gouge- and knife-worked, relief-carved, incised, and chip-carved (nineteenth century).

1

2

3

4

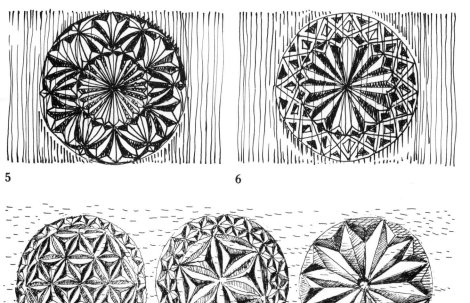

5

6

7

4. Sweden—hand mangle/beater detail; knife- and gouge-worked, relief-carved, incised, and chip-carved (nineteenth century).

5. Sweden—hand mangle/beater detail; gouge- and knife-worked, chip-carved (nineteenth century).

6. Sweden—hand mangle/beater detail; knife- and gouge-worked, chip-carved (nineteenth century).

7. England—panel detail; knife- and gouge-worked, deeply chip-carved (thirteenth century).

Moulds, Stamps, and Prints

1. England—butter print/press; gouge-worked, relief-carved so as to give a positive convex print (nineteenth century).

2. Sweden—cake/biscuit stamp; gouge-worked, relief-carved so as to give a convex print (nineteenth century).

3. England—butter print/stamp; gouge- and knife-worked, relief-carved so as to give a convex print (nineteenth century).

4. England—butter print/stamp; gouge- and knife-worked, relief-carved so as to give a convex print (nineteenth century).

1

2

3

4

5

6

7

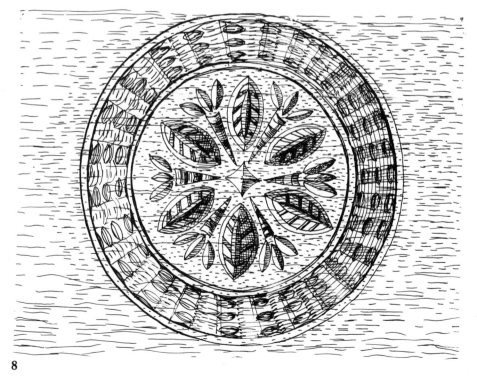

8

5. Poland, Silesia—gingerbread mould; knife- and gouge-worked, relief-carved (nineteenth century).

6. England—butter print; knife- and gouge-worked, relief-carved so as to give a raised print (early twentieth century?).

7. England—butter print; knife- and gouge-worked, relief-carved so as to give a raised print (nineteenth century).

8. England—butter print; knife- and gouge-worked, relief-carved so as to give a raised print (nineteenth century).

Flower Circles

1. England—detail from a "sunflower" design; worked with gouge and punch, gouge-carved in shallow relief (early seventeenth century).

2. England—detail from a strap-work panel design; gouge-worked, gouge-carved in shallow relief (seventeenth century).

3. England—detail from a pulpit door; gouge-worked, gouge-carved in shallow relief (early seventeenth century).

4. England—detail of box border strap-work design; gouge-worked, gouge-carved in shallow relief (seventeenth century).

1

2

3

4

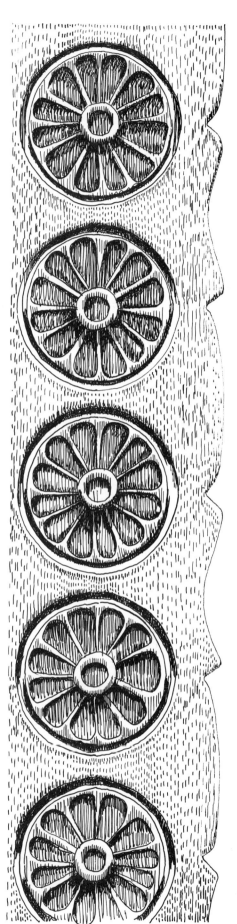

5. Portugal—detail from an ox yoke; gouge- and knife-worked, carved in shallow relief, and painted (early nineteenth century).

6. Portugal—detail from an ox yoke; gouge- and knife-worked, gouge-carved in shallow relief, detailed with a knife, and painted (nineteenth century).

5   6

Pierced Circles

1. Portugal—detail from an ox yoke; gouge- and knife-worked, gouge-carved, pierced (eighteenth century).

2. Sweden—detail from a distaff; knife-worked, whittled, pierced, and painted (nineteenth century).

3. Portugal—detail from an ox yoke; gouge- and knife-worked, relief-carved, pierced, and incised (eighteenth century).

4. Sweden—detail from a distaff; knife-worked, whittled, pierced, and chip-carved (nineteenth century).

5. Portugal—detail from a harness; gouge- and knife-worked, relief-carved, incised, pierced, and painted (eighteenth century).

1

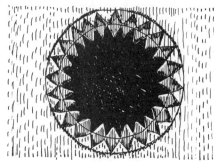

2

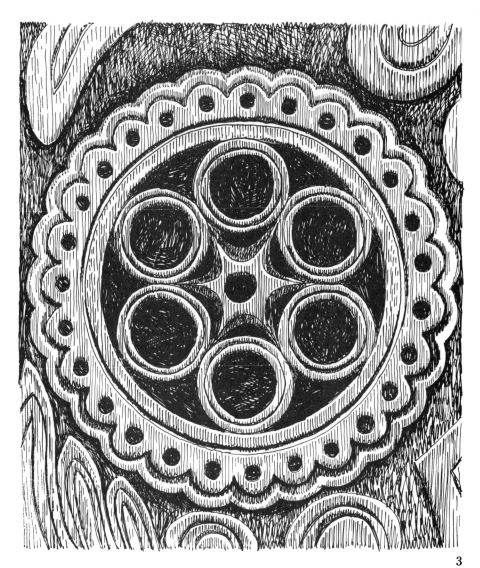

3

4

5

6

7

8

9

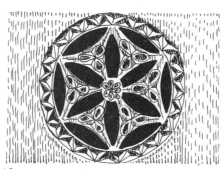

10

6. Portugal—detail from a harness; gouge- and knife-worked, relief-carved, incised, pierced, and painted (eighteenth century).

7. Portugal—detail from an ox yoke; gouge- and knife-worked, relief-carved, incised, pierced, and painted (eighteenth century).

8. England, Salisbury—detail from a dole cupboard; gouge-worked, deeply gouge-carved, and pierced (sixteenth century).

9. Sweden—detail from a distaff; knife-worked, whittled, pierced, and painted (nineteenth century).

10. Sweden—detail from a distaff; knife-worked, whittled, pierced, and painted (nineteenth century).

Knobs, Balls, and Beads

1. America, Mt. Lebanon, Pa.—Shaker rocking chair with "mushroom" finial detail; lathe-, saw-, and gouge-worked, turned, jointed, and carved (nineteenth century).

2. Sweden—knob and bead detail from a trinket box; worked with knife and gouge, gouge-carved, detailed with a knife, and painted (early nineteenth century).

3. Sweden—knob and bead detail from a trinket box; worked with knife and gouge, gouge-carved, and painted (early nineteenth century).

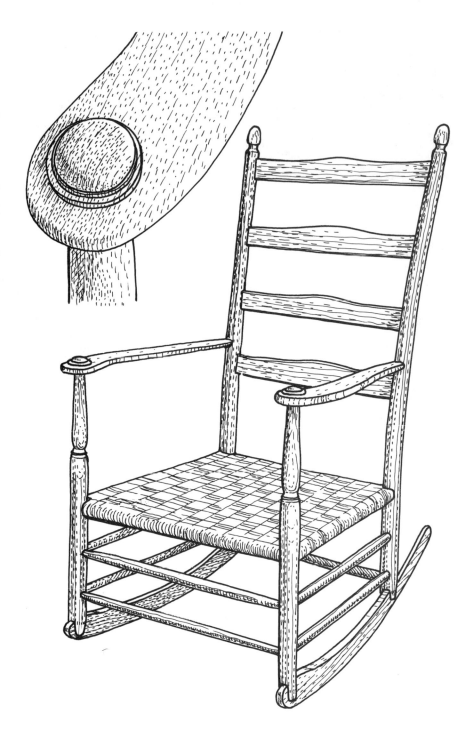

1

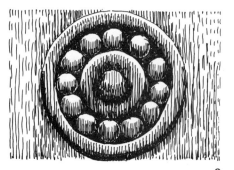

2

3

4

5

6

7

8

4. Sweden—a three-socket peg-leg chair with knobs and carving; lathe- and gouge-worked, turned, carved, and jointed (early eighteenth century).

5. Sweden—knob and bead detail from a trinket box; worked with knife and gouge, carved, undercut, and painted (early nineteenth century).

6. Sweden—tankard with knobs and handle; worked with gouge, drawknife, and lathe, barrel-built tankard, lathe-turned decorative knobs, and chip-carving (nineteenth century).

7. England—detail of chair back with knobs and carving; worked with gouge and lathe, jointed frame, lathe-turned knobs, spindles and split spindles, and shallow relief carving (mid-seventeenth century).

8. England—detail of chair back with knobs and carving; worked with gouge and lathe, lathe-turned knobs and gouge-cut shallow relief-carving (mid-seventeenth century).

Stencilled Circles

1. America—floor stencil detail; worked with oiled card stencil plate and paint, stencil-printed, and varnished (early nineteenth century).

2. England—detail of fireplace surround stencil; worked with oiled card stencil and paint, stencil-printed, and varnished (nineteenth century).

3. America—floor stencil detail; worked with oiled card stencil plate and paint, stencil-printed, and varnished (nineteenth century).

4. America—wall panel stencil detail; worked with oiled card stencil plate and paint, stencil-printed in two colors, and varnished (nineteenth century).

5. America—wall panel stencil detail; worked with oiled card stencil plate and paint, stencil-printed, and varnished (nineteenth century).

6. America—wall panel stencil detail; worked with oiled card stencil plate and paint, stencil-printed in two colors, and varnished (early nineteenth century).

7. America—floor stencil detail; worked with oiled card stencil plate and paint, stencil-printed, and varnished (early nineteenth century).

8. France—floor stencil detail; worked with oiled card stencil plate and paint, stencil-printed, and varnished (fifteenth century).

9. America—floor stencil detail; worked with oiled card stencil plate and paint, stencil-printed, and varnished (nineteenth century).

10. America—floor stencil detail; worked with oiled card stencil plate and paint, stencil-printed in two colors, and varnished (nineteenth century).

1

2

3

4

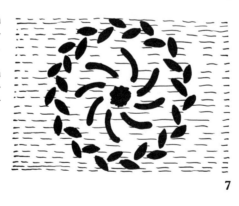

5

6

7

8

9

10

11. America—floor stencil detail; worked with oiled card stencil plate and earth colors, stencil-printed in two colors with two stencil plates, and then varnished (early nineteenth century).

11

Pennsylvanian American Hex

1. America—hex motif; painted (early nineteenth century).

2. America—hex motif; painted (early nineteenth century).

3. America—hex motif; painted (nineteenth century).

4. America—barn wall hex motif; painted (early nineteenth century).

5. America—barn wall hex motif; painted (early nineteenth century).

6. America—barn wall hex motif; painted (early nineteenth century).

7. America—barn wall hex motif; painted (nineteenth century).

8. America—hex motif; painted (nineteenth century).

9. America—barn wall hex motif; painted (early nineteenth century).

10. America—barn wall hex motif; painted (early nineteenth century).

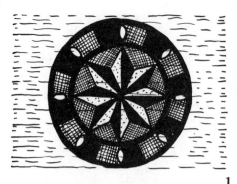

1

2

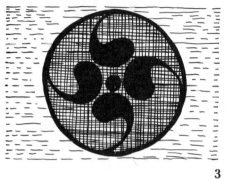

3

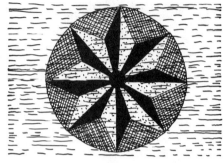

4

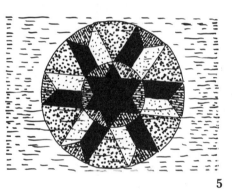

5

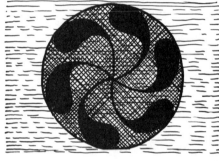

6

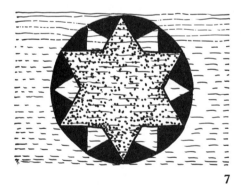

7

8

9

10

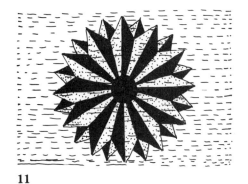

11

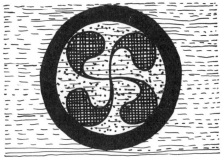

12

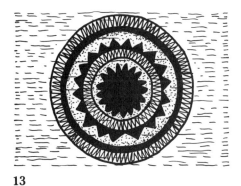

13

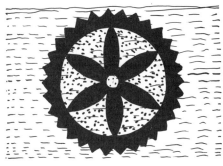

14

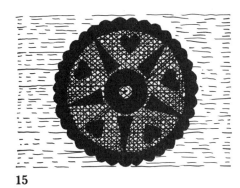

15

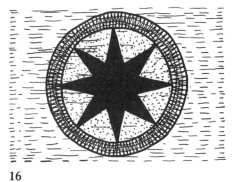

16

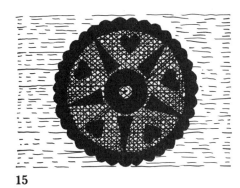

17

18

19

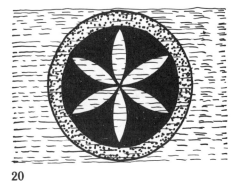

20

11. America—barn wall hex motif; painted (early nineteenth century).

12. America—barn wall hex motif; painted (early nineteenth century).

13. America—barn wall hex motif; painted (early nineteenth century).

14. America—barn wall hex motif; painted (early nineteenth century).

15. America—barn wall hex motif; painted (early nineteenth century).

16. America—barn wall hex motif; painted (early nineteenth century).

17. America—barn wall hex motif; painted (early nineteenth century).

18. America—barn wall hex motif; painted (early nineteenth century).

19. America—barn wall hex motif; painted (early nineteenth century).

20. America—barn wall hex motif; painted (early nineteenth century).

Suns and Flowers

1. America—inn sign; cut, carved, and painted (early nineteenth century).

2. Switzerland—inn sign; painted (early eighteenth century).

3. America—spoon holder detail; gouge- and knife-worked, gouge-carved, and chip-carved (late eighteenth century).

4. Sweden—cake stamp; knife-worked, whittled, and chip-carved (nineteenth century).

5. Italy, Sardinia—chest detail; gouge- and knife-worked, carved in shallow relief (seventeenth century).

6. Italy, Sicily—butter stamp; knife-worked, whittled in low relief (nineteenth century).

7. Italy, Sicily—butter stamp; knife-worked, carved in low relief (nineteenth century).

8. America—chest detail, sunflower motif; gouge-worked, carved in shallow relief, punch-textured ground (late seventeenth century).

9. America, Connecticut—chest detail, sunflower motif; gouge- and punch-worked, relief-carved in shallow relief with a punch-textured ground (early eighteenth century).

80

10

11

10. England—inn sign; painted and gilded (eighteenth century).

11. England, Norwich—inn sign; gouge- and knife-worked, gouge-carved in deep relief, pierced, and painted (eighteenth century).

Chip-Carved Circles and Zigzags

1. Holland—clothes beater detail; knife-worked, chip-carved, and incised (eighteenth century).

2. Yugoslavia—detail from a spinning spindle; knife-worked, chip-carved, and incised (eighteenth century).

1

2

3. Italy—detail from a clothes beater; knife-worked, chip-carved, and incised (eighteenth century).

3

French Circles

1. France—cupboard detail; worked with knife and gouge, relief-carved, and incised (early nineteenth century).

2. France—cupboard detail; worked with knife and gouge, relief-carved, and incised (early nineteenth century).

3. France—detail from a bride's chest; knife- and gouge-worked, relief-carved, and incised (seventeenth century).

4. France—detail from a small steam-bent basket; knife-worked and whittled (nineteenth century).

5. France—detail from a large carved chest; knife- and gouge-worked, relief-carved to shallow relief, and incised (early seventeenth century).

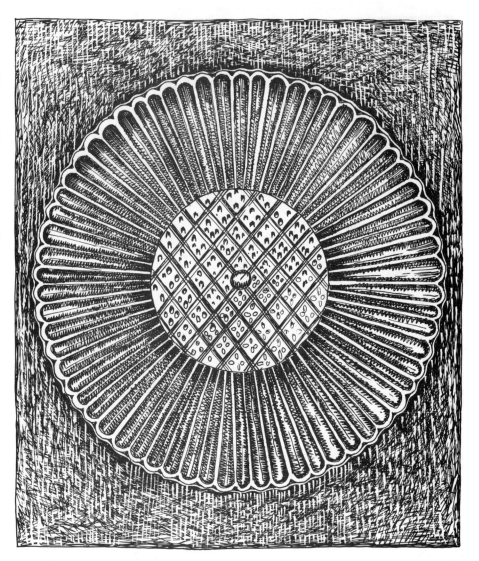

1

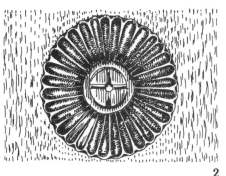

2

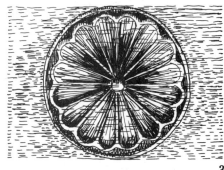

3

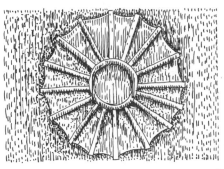

4

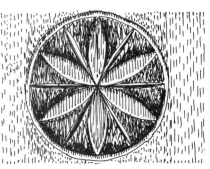

5

6

7

8

9

10

6. France—detail from a lace winder; knife-worked, whittled, pierced, and chip-carved (late eighteenth century).

7. France—detail from a lace winder; knife-worked, whittled, pierced, and chip-carved (late eighteenth century).

8. France—detail from a chest; knife- and gouge-worked, carved in shallow relief, and incised (seventeenth century).

9. France—detail from a large chest; gouge- and knife-worked, relief-carved, and incised (seventeenth century).

10. France—detail from a large chest; gouge- and knife-worked, deep relief-carved, and incised (seventeenth century).

Twined and Knotted Circles

1. France—detail from a small chest; gouge- and knife-worked, and chip-carved (seventeenth century).

2. Iceland—detail from a spinning whorl; knife-worked, shallow relief-carved, pierced, and incised (eighteenth century).

3. Holland—detail from a spoon rack; knife-worked, whittled, and pierced (nineteenth century).

4. Iceland—detail from a box lid; knife-worked, incised, and chip-carved (late seventeenth century).

5. France—detail from a lace winder; knife-worked, incised, and chip-carved (eighteenth century).

2

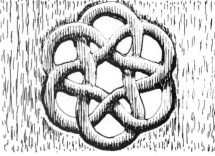

3

4

5

1

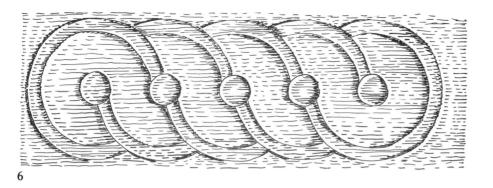

6

7

8

6. Sweden—detail from a mangle board/ beater; gouge-worked, and carved in very shallow relief (nineteenth century).

7. France—detail from a chest; knife- and gouge-worked, chip-carved, and incised (seventeenth century).

8. England(?)—detail from a "darning" foot; knife-worked, chip-carved, and incised (mid-nineteenth century).

Chapter Three

Twined Forms

Twined Knots

1. Sweden—detail from a chest; knife-worked, incised (early seventeenth century).

2. Sweden—detail from a chest; knife-worked and incised (early seventeenth century).

3. Switzerland—detail from a chest; knife-worked and incised (late sixteenth century).

4. Iceland—detail from a hand mangle/beater; knife- and gouge-worked, shallow relief-carved, and incised (eighteenth century).

5. Iceland—detail from a hand mangle/beater; knife- and gouge-worked, shallow relief-carved, and gouge-worked (eighteenth century).

6. Sweden—detail from a chest; knife- and gouge-worked, shallow relief-carved, and incised (late nineteenth century).

1

2

3

4

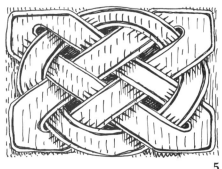

5

6

7. Sweden—detail from a cake stamp; knife-worked and incised (eighteenth century).

8. Germany—slab-back chair detail; knife-, drill-, and gouge-worked, and pierced (eighteenth century).

9. Norway—bed end detail; knife-worked and incised (seventeenth century).

10. Sweden—box lid; gouge- and knife-worked, carved in shallow relief, and incised (eighteenth century).

Knots and Weaves

1. Sweden—detail from a saddle/harness; knife- and gouge-worked, shallow relief-carved, and incised (eighteenth century).

2. Romania—detail from a chest; knife-worked and incised (nineteenth century).

3. Yugoslavia—detail from a distaff; knife-worked and incised (nineteenth century).

4. Yugoslavia—detail from a distaff; knife-worked and incised (nineteenth century).

5. Yugoslavia—detail from a carved distaff; knife-worked and incised (early nineteenth century).

6. Poland—detail from a ladle; knife- and gouge-worked, chip-carved, and incised (early nineteenth century).

7. Russia—detail on a birch-bark container; knife- and gouge-worked, deeply incised, and chip-carved (nineteenth century).

8. Poland—detail from a washing paddle; knife-worked and incised (nineteenth century).

9. Sweden—detail from a shaving box; knife-worked and deeply incised (late eighteenth century).

10. Yugoslavia—detail from a distaff; knife-worked, deeply incised, and shallow scratched (early nineteenth century).

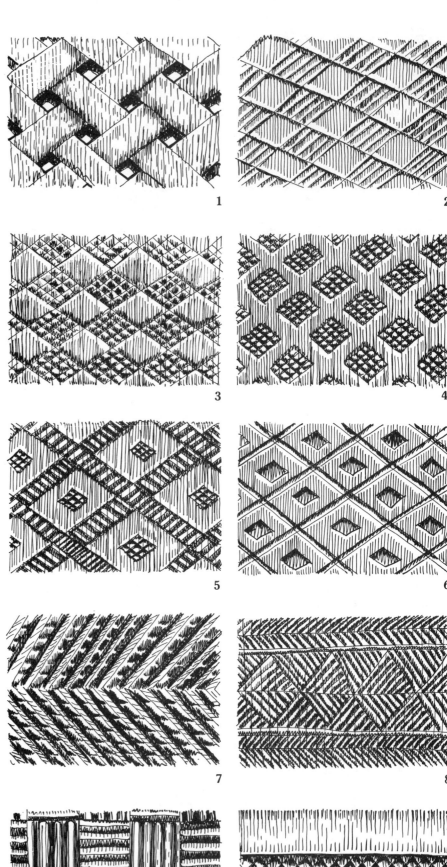

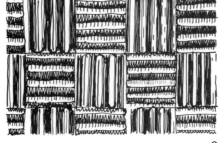

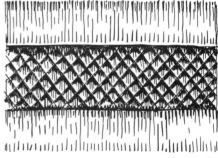

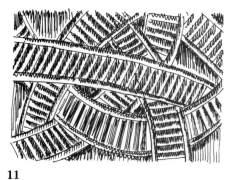

11

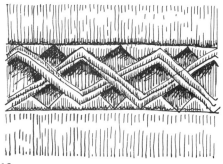

12

13

14

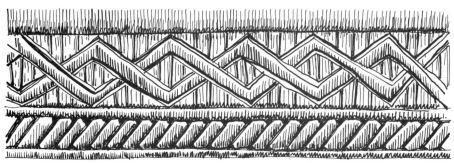

15

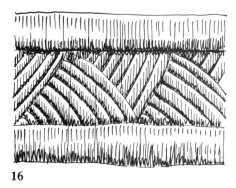

16

17

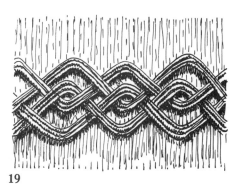

18

19

11. Sweden—detail from a love spoon; knife-worked, deeply incised, and scratched (eighteenth century).

12. Lithuania—detail from a distaff; knife-worked and deeply incised (nineteenth century).

13. Sweden—detail from a box; knife-worked, painted, and incised (eighteenth century).

14. Norway—detail from a door post; knife- and gouge-worked, relief-carved, and incised (fourteenth century).

15. Sweden—detail from a bowl; knife- and gouge-worked, incised with a V-gouge, and scratch-carved (seventeenth century).

16. Sweden—detail from a weaving tool; knife- and gouge-worked and incised (eighteenth century).

17. Germany—detail from a letter rack; knife- and gouge-worked, incised, and chip-carved (nineteenth century).

18. Sweden—detail from a distaff; knife- and gouge-worked, relief-carved, pierced, incised, and painted (early nineteenth century).

19. Sweden—detail from a box; knife- and gouge-worked, relief-carved, and incised (thirteenth century).

Seventeenth-Century English

1. England, Yorkshire(?)—chair back detail; gouge and knife work, carved in shallow relief, sawn, and knife-worked (seventeenth century).

2. England—box detail; gouge and knife work, carved in shallow relief, punch-textured ground, and knife-incised (seventeenth century).

3. England—hanging shelf border detail; knife and gouge work, shallow relief carved with a smooth ground (seventeenth century).

4. England—detail on a court cupboard; knife and gouge work, shallow relief-carved strapwork with a smooth punch-textured ground (seventeenth century).

5. England—detail from a Bible box; knife- and gouge-worked, shallow relief-carved with a flat ground, and incised (seventeenth century).

6. England—detail from a cupboard; knife and gouge work, carved in shallow relief with a level punch-textured ground (seventeenth century).

1

2

3

4

5

6

94

7

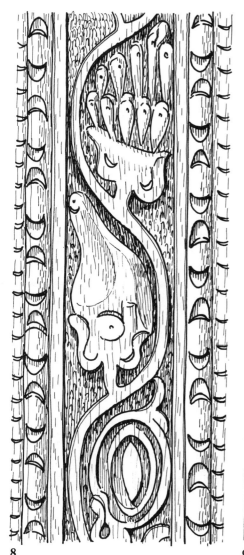

8　　　　　　　　　9

7. England—detail from a hanging shelf; knife- and gouge-worked, shallow relief-carved with a level punch-textured ground (seventeenth century).

8. England—detail from a chest; knife- and gouge-worked, shallow relief-carving with a punch-textured ground (seventeenth century).

9. England, Quenby Hall, Leicestershire—detail from a panel; knife- and gouge-worked, shallow relief-carved with a smooth ground (seventeenth century).

Painted and Scratch-Carved

1. Romania—detail from a chest; knife-worked, painted, and scratch-carved (nineteenth century).

2. Romania—detail from a chest; knife-worked, painted, and scratch-carved (nineteenth century).

3. Romania—detail from a chest; knife-worked, painted, and scratch-carved (nineteenth century).

4. Yugoslavia—detail from a beaker; knife-worked, painted, and scratch-carved (nineteenth century).

5. Yugoslavia—detail from a beaker; knife-worked, painted, and scratch-carved (nineteenth century).

1

2

3

4

5

6

7

8

9

10

6. Yugoslavia—detail from a whetstone holder; knife-worked, painted, and scratch-carved (nineteenth century).

7. Romania—detail from a chest; knife-worked, painted, and scratch-carved (seventeenth century).

8. Yugoslavia—detail from a beaker; knife-worked, painted, and scratch-carved (nineteenth century).

9. Yugoslavia—detail from a distaff; knife-worked, painted, and scratch-carved (nineteenth century).

10. Yugoslavia—detail from a distaff; knife-worked, painted, and scratch-carved (nineteenth century).

97

Twists and Turns

1. Sweden—a flour spoon; knife-worked and gouged, whittled, and carved with a fluted twist (nineteenth century).

2. America, Mt. Lebanon, Pa.—a Shaker rocker armchair; lathe-, gouge-, and knife-worked, turned on the lathe, "rope twist" carved, and jointed (nineteenth century).

1

2

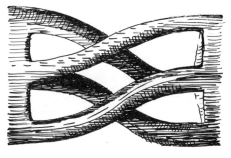

4

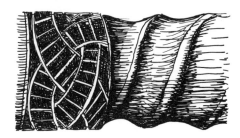

5

6

7

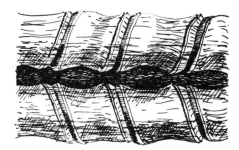

8

3. Finland—a weaving/spinning tool; knife- and gouge-worked, whittled, gouge-carved, pierced, and chip-carved (eighteenth century).

4. Sweden—detail from a candlestick; knife- and gouge-worked, carved, and pierced (eighteenth century).

5. Sweden—detail from a love spoon; knife-worked, whittled, painted, incised, and carved with a fluted twist (eighteenth century).

6. Finland—detail from a distaff; knife-worked, whittled, and chip-carved, carved with a slow pierced twist (eighteenth century).

7. England—detail from a pair of nutcrackers; knife-worked, whittled, and chip-carved with an incised twist (nineteenth century).

8. Sweden—detail from a mangle/pressing board; knife- and gouge-worked, carved, and incised (late eighteenth century).

Twists and Twines

1. Sweden—detail from a wool box/chest; saw-, knife-, and gouge-worked, carved, pierced, incised, and jointed (thirteenth century).

2. Sweden—detail from a cupboard; knife- and gouge-worked, carved, pierced, and painted (mid-nineteenth century).

3. Switzerland—detail from a chest; knife- and gouge-worked, shallow relief-carved, and incised (sixteenth century).

4. Sweden—detail from a cupboard; knife- and gouge-worked, carved in shallow relief, and painted (eighteenth century).

5. Sweden—detail from a cupboard; knife- and gouge-worked, carved in shallow relief, and painted (mid-nineteenth century).

1

2

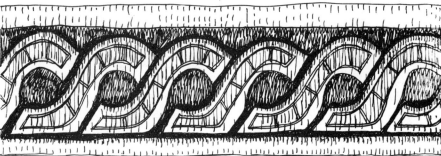

3

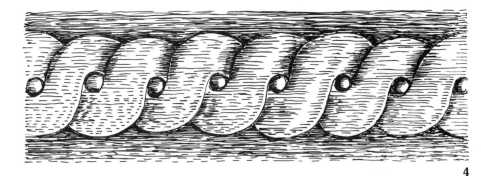

4

5

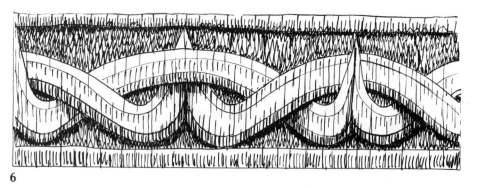

6

7

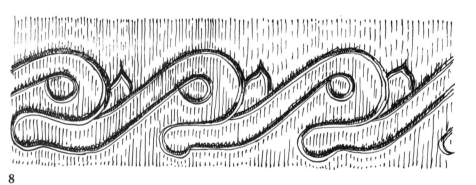

8

9

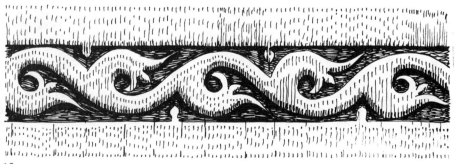

10

6. Sweden—detail from a cupboard; knife- and gouge-worked, carved in shallow relief with a flat textured ground (sixteenth century).

7. Sweden—detail from a box; knife- and gouge-worked, and incised (eighteenth century).

8. Sweden—detail from a box; knife- and gouge-worked, and incised (eighteenth century).

9. Switzerland—detail from a chest; knife- and gouge-worked, carved in shallow relief with a flat ground (sixteenth century).

10. Sweden—detail from a curtain/crown rail; knife- and gouge-worked, relief-carved with a flat ground (mid-eighteenth century).

Icelandic
Twined

1. Iceland—bed board detail; knife- and gouge-worked, shallow relief-carved (eighteenth century).

2. Iceland—box detail; knife-worked, carved in shallow relief (seventeenth century?).

3. Iceland—bed board detail; knife-worked, relief-carved, and incised (eighteenth century).

1

2

3

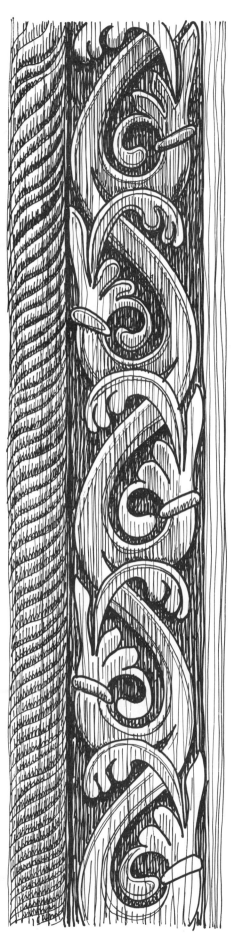

5

6

4. Iceland—hand mangle detail; knife-worked, flat-face relief-carved, and incised (eighteenth century).

5. Iceland—box detail; knife-worked, shallow relief-carved, and incised (eighteenth century).

6. Iceland—box detail; knife-worked, shallow relief-carved, and incised (seventeenth century?).

7. Iceland—box detail; knife-worked and incised (seventeenth century?).

4   7

Scandinavian Twined

1. Sweden—detail from a spoon handle; knife-worked, pierced (seventeenth century?).

2. Norway—post detail; knife- and gouge-worked, carved in shallow relief (seventeenth century?).

3. Iceland—box detail; knife-worked, carved in shallow relief (early nineteenth century).

4. Iceland—bed detail; knife- and gouge-worked, flat-face relief-carved (seventeenth century).

5. Iceland—bed board detail; knife- and gouge-worked, flat-face relief-carved (eighteenth century).

6. Iceland—box detail; knife- and gouge-worked, shallow relief worked, and incised (eighteenth century?).

1

2

3

4

5

6

7

8

9

10

11

7. Sweden—cabinet detail; knife- and gouge-worked, carved in shallow relief, and painted (seventeenth century).

8. Iceland—detail from a bed board; knife- and gouge-worked, carved in deep relief (eighteenth century).

9. Iceland—box detail; knife-worked, carved in shallow relief (seventeenth century).

10. Iceland—bed board detail; knife- and gouge-worked, pierced, and carved (seventeenth century?).

11. Iceland—detail from a box; knife- and gouge-worked, relief-carved, and incised (seventeenth century).

Magic Knots

1. Iceland—cupboard door; knife- and gouge-worked, deep relief carving (seventeenth century).

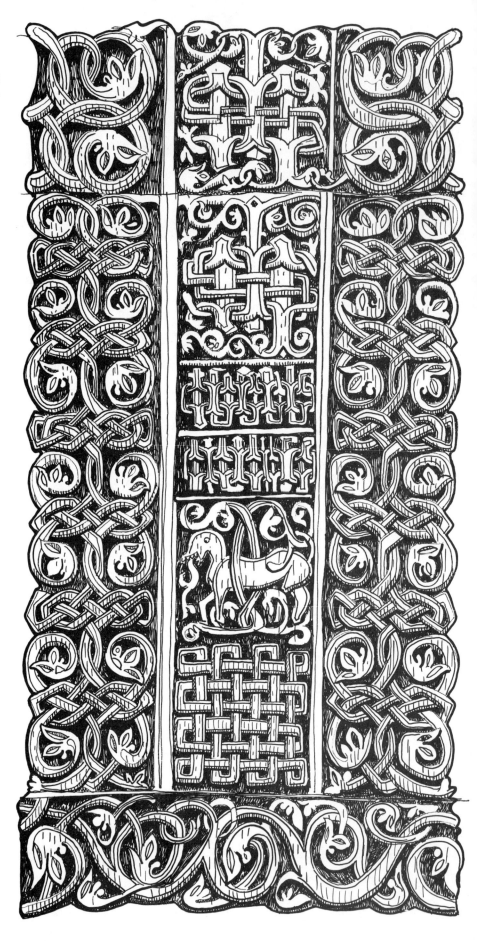

1

2. Iceland—cupboard door; knife- and gouge-worked, deep relief carving (seventeenth century).

2

Fairground Twined

1. America—detail from C. W. Parker's "Electric Theatre"; knife- and gouge-worked, carved, and gilded (late nineteenth century).

2. England—detail from C. J. Spooner's switchback ride; knife- and gouge-worked, relief-carved, and painted (early twentieth century).

3. America—detail from C. W. Parker's "Electric Theatre"; knife- and gouge-worked, carved, and gilded (early twentieth century).

4. Belgium—detail from a roundabout gondola; knife- and gouge-worked, shallow relief-carved, and gilded (early twentieth century).

5. England—detail from a roundabout fascia board; knife- and gouge-worked, carved, and painted (early twentieth century).

6. England—detail from C. J. Spooner's motor car switchback ride; knife- and gouge-worked, carved, and painted (early twentieth century).

1

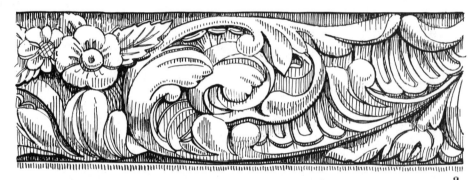

2

3

4

5

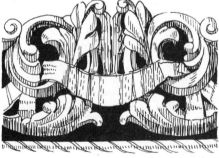

6

7

8

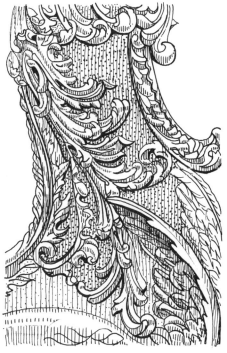

9

10

7. England—roundabout detail; knife- and gouge-worked, carved, and painted (early twentieth century).

8. England—detail from a galloper's body, carved by J. R. Anderson; knife- and gouge-worked, carved, and painted (early twentieth century).

9. England—detail from a galloper, carved by J. R. Anderson; knife- and gouge-worked, carved, and painted (early twentieth century).

10. America—detail from McIllion's chariot ride; knife- and gouge-worked, carved, and painted (early twentieth century).

Twined and Painted

1. Denmark—detail from a cupboard; painted (nineteenth century).

2. Germany, Bavaria—detail from an armoire panel; painted (seventeenth century).

3. Norway—detail from a door panel; painted (eighteenth century).

4. Sweden, Smaland(?)—detail from a trinket box; painted (nineteenth century).

5. Germany, Berchtesgaden—detail from a bentwood box; painted (eighteenth century).

6. Italy—detail from a yoke; painted (nineteenth century).

1

2

6

7. Holland—detail from a folding table; painted (eighteenth century).

Twined Inlay

1. England—armchair, back panel detail; thick wood inlay (early seventeenth century).

2. England—detail from a backgammon board, repeat design; thick wood inlay (early seventeenth century).

1

2

3

3. England—armchair, back panel detail; thick wood inlay (early seventeenth century).

4. England—chest detail; thick wood inlay (seventeenth century).

4

113

Twined
Stencilled

1. America, Boston—by W. P. Eaton, a chair back detail; oiled card stencil plate, varnish and gold powder, stencil-printed with varnish, and dusted (nineteenth century).

2. America, Boston—by W. P. Eaton, a chair design; oiled card stencil, varnish and gold powder, stencil-printed with varnish, and dusted with gold (nineteenth century).

3. America, Boston—by W. P. Eaton, a chair design; oiled card, varnish and gold powder, stencil-printed with varnish, and gold dusted (nineteenth century).

1

2

3

4

5

6

7

4. America, Mass.—chair detail; oiled card varnish and gold powder, stencil-printed with varnish, and gold dusted (nineteenth century).

5. America, Boston—by W. P. Eaton, chair rail design; oiled card, varnish and gold powder, stencil-printed with varnish, and gold dusted (nineteenth century).

6. America, Boston—by W. P. Eaton, chair back design; oiled card, varnish and gold powder, stencil-printed with varnish, and gold dusted (nineteenth century).

7. America, Boston—by W. P. Eaton, chair back design; oil card stencil plate, varnish and gold powder, stencil-printed with varnish, and gold dusted (nineteenth century).

115

Stencilled and Painted

1. America, Dauphin County, Pa.—dower chest detail; painted (eighteenth century).

2. America, Newton, Mass.—floor detail; oiled card stencil plate and paint, stencil-printed, and varnished (late eighteenth century).

1

2

3

4

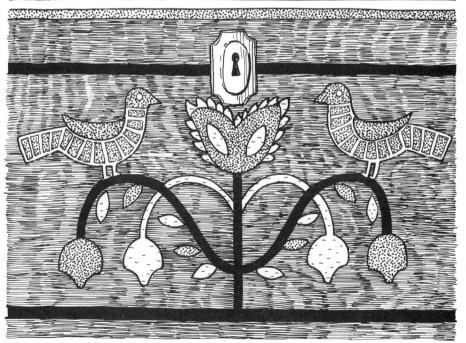

5

3. America, New Hampshire—by Moses Eaton, wall panel detail; oiled card stencil plate and painted, stencil-printed (early nineteenth century).

4. America, Pennsylvania—wall panel detail; painted (early nineteenth century).

5. America, Snyder County, Pa.—detail from a chest of drawers; painted (nineteenth century).

French Twists and Knots

1. France—detail from a bride's chest; worked with gouge and knife, and relief-carved (seventeenth century).

2. France—detail from a bride's chest; worked with gouge and knife, and relief-carved (seventeenth century).

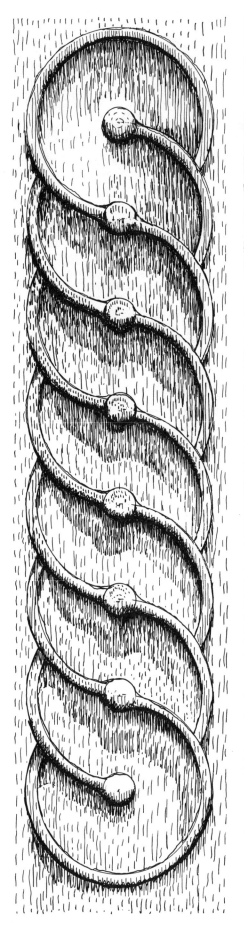

1

2

3. France—detail from a bride's chest; worked with gouge and knife, relief-carved, and chip-carved (seventeenth century).

4. France—detail from a chest; worked with knife and gouge, relief-carved, and incised (mid-seventeenth century).

3

4

119

Twined Low Relief

1. Germany, Friesland—box lid detail; knife- and gouge-worked, carved in low relief with a flat ground and painted (eighteenth century).

2. Portugal—detail from a double ox yoke; knife- and gouge-worked, carved in low relief with a flat ground, pierced, chip-carved, incised, and painted (nineteenth century).

1

2

3

3. Iceland—detail from a bed headboard; knife- and gouge-worked, carved in relief with a flat ground (nineteenth century).

4. Norway—a dresser; knife- and gouge-worked, carved in low and high relief, undercut, carved in the round, pierced, and painted (late eighteenth century).

4

Chapter Four

Plant Forms

Naïve Flowers

1. Sweden—detail from a beer stoop; hot iron, poker work (nineteenth century).

2. England, Cheshire—detail of a timber-framed building; saw and gouge, massive timbers cut, and jointed (sixteenth century).

3. Yugoslavia—detail from a herdsman's beaker; knife-worked, incised, and painted (nineteenth century).

4. Sweden—detail from a tankard; hot iron, poker work (nineteenth century).

5. England, Cheshire, Little Moreton Hall—detail of timber-framed house; saw and gouge, massive timbers cut, and jointed (sixteenth century).

6. Sweden—detail from a tankard; hot iron, poker work (nineteenth century).

7. Sweden, Jamtland(?)—detail from a flour box; hot iron, poker work (nineteenth century).

1

2

3

4

6

7

124

8

10

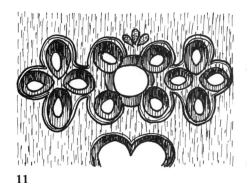

11

9

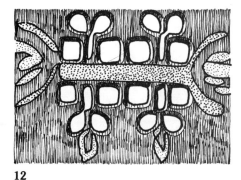

12

14

13

8. Sweden, Northern Jamtland(?)—detail from a butter mould; gouge- and knife-worked, carved in shallow relief so as to give a proud/convex stamped image (nineteeth century).

9. Germany—detail from a letter rack; gouge- and knife-worked, chip-carved, and incised (nineteenth century).

10. Sweden, Oland—detail from a hand mangle/press/beater; knife- and gouge-worked, chip-carved, and incised (nineteenth century).

11. Sweden, Uppland—detail from a distaff; knife- and gouge-worked, pierced, incised, and painted (nineteenth century).

12. Sweden, Dalarne—detail from a spinning tool; knife-worked, pierced, incised, and painted (nineteenth century).

13. Sweden, Dalarne—detail from a spinning tool; knife-worked, pierced, and painted (nineteenth century).

14. Sweden, Dalarne—detail from a spinning tool; knife-worked, pierced, and painted (nineteenth century).

125

Chip-Carved Flowers

1

2

1. Sweden—detail from a weaving beater; knife-worked, chip-carved, and incised (nineteenth century).

2. Transylvania—detail from a grindstone sheath; knife-worked, chip-carved, and incised (nineteenth century).

3. Austria—detail from a clothes beater; knife-worked, chip-carved, and incised (eighteenth century).

4. England—detail from a panel; knife-worked, chip-carved, and incised (nineteenth century).

5. Germany—detail from a clothes beater; knife-worked, chip-carved, and incised (eighteenth century?).

3

4

5

6

7

8

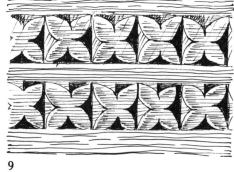

9

10

6. Germany—detail from a letter rack; knife-worked, chip-carved, and incised (nineteenth century).

7. Germany—detail from a flax beater; knife-worked, chip-carved, and incised (eighteenth century).

8. America, Pennsylvania—detail from a candle box; knife-worked, chip-carved, incised, and painted (early nineteenth century).

9. England—detail from a panel; knife- and gouge-worked, chip-carved, and incised (nineteenth century).

10. America, Pennsylvania—detail from a candle box; knife-worked, chip-carved, incised, and painted (early nineteenth century).

Painted Fireboards and Panels

1. America, Belle Mead, N.J.—detail from a panelled door surround; painted and grained (early nineteenth century).

2. America, Belle Mead, N.J.—detail from a panelled door surround; painted and grained (early nineteenth century).

3. America, Brookfield, Mass.—detail from a fireboard; painted (early nineteenth century).

1

2

3

4

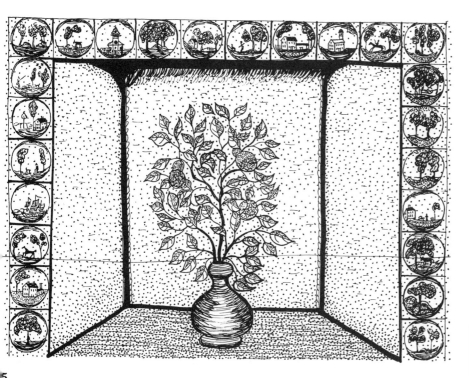

4. France, Alsace—a marriage memento panel; painted (nineteenth century).

5. America—a fireboard in perspective with tile effect; painted (early nineteenth century).

5

129

Strap-Work and Flat Relief

1. Sweden, Halland—detail from a cupboard; knife- and gouge-worked, carved in shallow relief with a flat ground, painted (seventeenth century).

2. America, New England—detail from a Bible box; knife- and gouge-worked, strapwork carved in low relief, with a flat ground (seventeenth century).

3. England—detail from a court cupboard; knife- and gouge-worked, strap-work carved in low/shallow relief with a flat ground (seventeenth century).

4. England—detail from a court cupboard; knife- and gouge-worked, strap-work carved in low/shallow relief with a flat ground (seventeenth century).

5. England—detail from a table settle; knife- and gouge-worked, carved in low relief with a flat ground (seventeenth century).

6. England—detail from a table settle; knife- and gouge-worked, carved in low relief with a flat ground (seventeenth century).

1

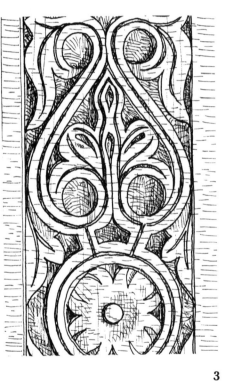

2

4

3

5

6

130

7. Sweden, Smaland (?)—detail from a corner cupboard; knife- and gouge-worked, carved in shallow relief (eighteenth century).

8. Sweden, Blekinge—detail from a corner cupboard; knife- and gouge-worked, carved in shallow relief (nineteenth century).

9. Iceland—detail from a knitting needle case; knife- and gouge-worked, shallow relief-carved with a flat ground (eighteenth century).

10. Sweden, Angermanland—detail from a corner cupboard; knife- and gouge-worked, carved in shallow relief with a flat ground (nineteenth century).

11. Iceland—box detail; knife- and gouge-worked, carved in shallow relief, incised, and chip-carved (eighteenth century).

12. England, Quenby Hall, Leicestershire—detail from a panel; knife- and gouge-worked, strap-work carved in shallow relief with a flat ground (seventeenth century).

13. Iceland—detail from a hand mangle; knife- and gouge-worked, carved in shallow relief, slightly undercut and chip-carved (eighteenth century).

14. Iceland—detail from a knitting needle case; knife-worked, carved in shallow relief, and incised (eighteenth century).

131

American Gold-Stencilled

1. America, Connecticut—detail from a shelf clock; oiled card stencil plate gold/bronze powder, and varnished, painted black, stencil-printed with varnish, and powder-dusted (nineteenth century).

2. America, Connecticut—detail from a shelf clock; oiled card stencil plate gold/bronze powder, and varnished, painted black, stencil-printed with varnish, and powder-dusted (nineteenth century).

3. America—detail from a box; oiled card stencil plate gold/bronze powder, and varnished, painted black, stencil-printed with varnish, and powder-dusted (nineteenth century).

4. America—chair detail; oiled card stencil plate gold/bronze powder, and varnished, painted black, stencil-printed with varnish, and powder-dusted (nineteenth century).

5. America—Ransom Cook stencil detail; oiled card stencil plate gold/bronze powder, and varnished, painted black, stencil-printed with varnish, and powder-dusted (nineteenth century).

6. America—Ransom Cook stencil detail; oiled card stencil plate gold/bronze powder, and varnished, painted black, stencil-printed with varnish, and powder-dusted (nineteenth century).

7. America—chair stencil detail; oiled card stencil plate gold/bronze powder, and varnished, painted black, stencil-printed with varnish, and powder-dusted (nineteenth century).

1

2

3

4

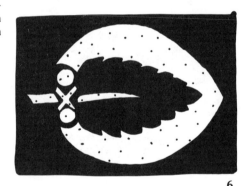

5

6

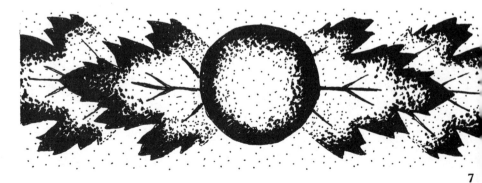

7

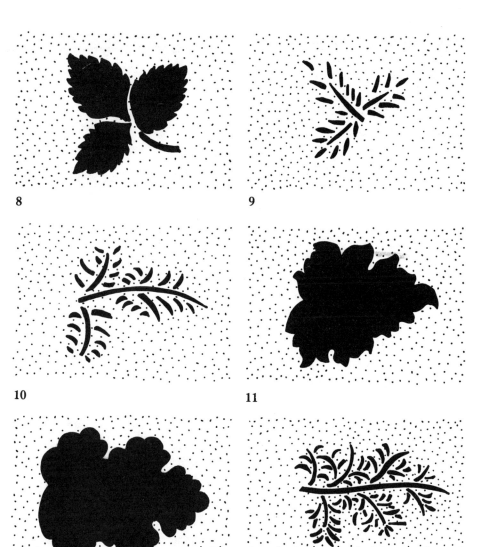

8. America—furniture stencil plate detail for gold-powder stencil; oiled card (nineteenth century).

9. America—furniture stencil plate detail for gold-powder stencil; oiled card (nineteenth century).

10. America—furniture stencil plate detail for gold-powder stencil; oiled card (nineteenth century).

11. America—furniture stencil plate detail for gold-powder stencil; oiled card (nineteenth century).

12. America—furniture stencil plate detail for gold-powder stencil; oiled card (nineteenth century).

13. America—furniture stencil plate detail for gold-powder stencil; oiled card (nineteenth century).

14. America—stencil detail for a picture frame; painted black, stencil-printed with varnish, and gold-powder-dusted (nineteenth century).

15. America—border stencil using three-leaf repeats, painted black, stencil-printed with varnish, and gold-dusted (nineteenth century).

American Stencilled-Leaf

1. America—chair stencil detail; black-painted, stencil-printed with varnish, and gold-dusted (nineteenth century).

2. America—stencilled box detail; black-painted, stencil-printed with varnish, and gold-dusted (nineteenth century).

3. America—stencilled picture surround detail; black-painted, stencil-printed with varnish, and gold-dusted (nineteenth century).

4. America—stencilled box detail; black-painted, stencil-printed with varnish, and gold-dusted (nineteenth century).

5. America—stencilled picture surround detail; black-painted, stencil-printed with varnish, and gold-dusted (nineteenth century).

6. America—stencilled box detail; black-painted, stencil-printed with varnish, and gold-dusted (nineteenth century).

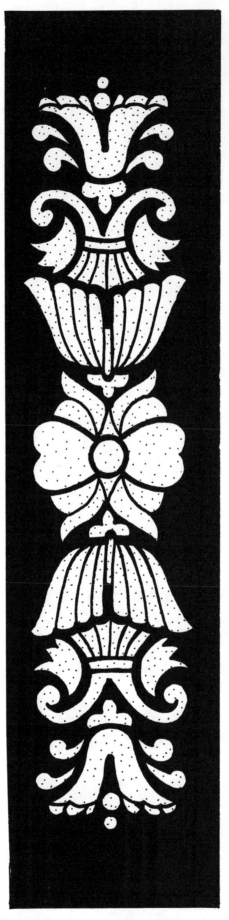

1

2

3

4

5

6

7

8

9

10

11

12

7. America—stencilled box detail; black-painted, stencil-printed with varnish, and gold-dusted (nineteenth century).

8. America—by Gildersleeve, stencil plate detail; oiled card (nineteenth century).

9. America—by Gildersleeve, stencil plate detail; oiled card (nineteenth century).

10. America—by Gildersleeve, stencil plate detail; oiled card (nineteenth century).

11. America—by Gildersleeve, stencil plate detail; oiled card (nineteenth century).

12. America—by Gildersleeve, stencil plate detail; oiled card (nineteenth century).

Painted Tulips

1. America, Ohio—chest detail; painted (nineteenth century).

2. Poland, Katowice Province—hope chest detail; painted (nineteenth century).

3. America—detail from a Pennsylvanian German dower chest; painted (eighteenth century).

4. Germany, Thuringia—detail from a cake tray; painted (nineteenth century).

5. America, Berks County, Pa.—detail from a dower chest; painted (nineteenth century).

6. Germany, Angeln—detail from a chest; painted (nineteenth century).

7. America—detail from a Pennsylvanian German dower chest; painted (nineteenth century).

8. Romania—detail from a bride's chest; painted (nineteenth century).

9. America—detail from a Pennsylvanian chest; painted (eighteenth century).

10. America—detail from a Pennsylvanian dower chest; painted (eighteenth century).

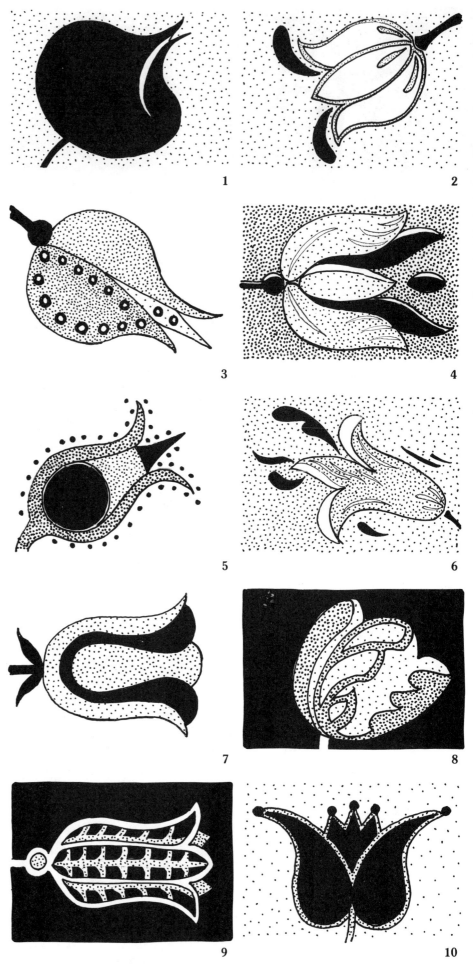

136

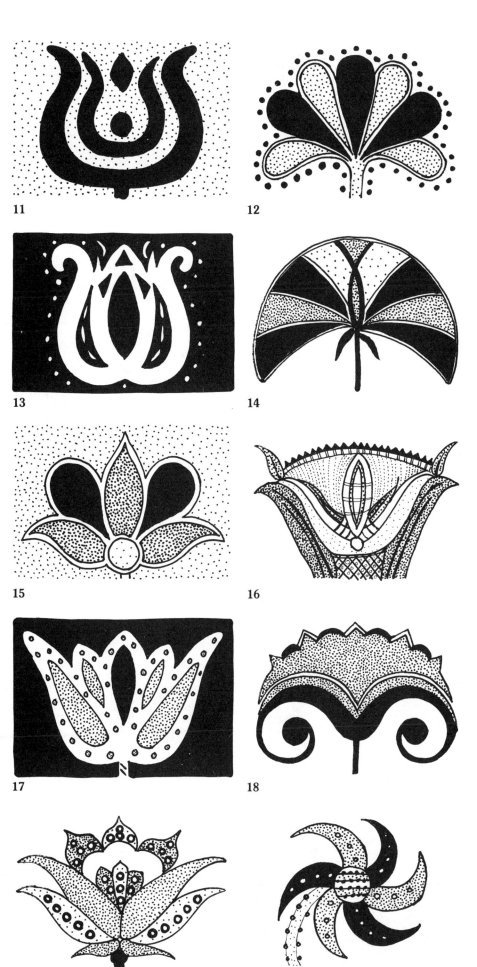

11. America—detail from a Pennsylvanian box; painted (nineteenth century).

12. America, Berks County, Pa.—detail from a dower chest (nineteenth century).

13. America—detail from a Pennsylvanian German dower chest; painted (nineteenth century).

14. America—detail from a Pennsylvanian dower chest; painted (nineteenth century).

15. America—detail from a Pennsylvanian German dower chest (eighteenth century).

16. Sweden, Dalarna—detail from a cupboard; painted (eighteenth century).

17. America, New England—detail from a chest of drawers; painted (seventeenth century).

18. America, Lancaster County, Pa.—detail from a dower chest; painted (eighteenth century).

19. America—detail from a Pennsylvanian German dower chest; painted by Christian Selzer (?) (eighteenth century).

20. America—detail from a Pennsylvanian German chest; painted (eighteenth century).

Brush Strokes

1. Sweden, Skane—corner cupboard detail; painted with bold brush strokes (nineteenth century).

2. Norway, Hardanger—carved beer bowl detail; painted with bold brush strokes (nineteenth century).

3. America—detail from a Pennsylvania Dutch tray; painted (nineteenth century).

4. Norway—detail from a chest; painted in the rosemaling tradition/technique (eighteenth century).

1

2

3

4

138

6

7

5

8

9

5. Sweden, Mora, Dalarne—detail from a standing clock panel; painted with fine-line brush strokes and infill (nineteenth century).

6. Poland, Kuyavia—detail from a chest; painted (nineteenth century).

7. Sweden, Dalarne—detail from a hanging cradle; a painted repeat design (nineteenth century).

8. Sweden, Bohuslan Province—detail from a chest; painted (eighteenth century).

9. Norway, Hallingdal—detail from a coopered beer jug; painted with broad flourish strokes (nineteenth century).

English Canal Art

1. England, Rugby—rose and leaf design by Dennis Clark; painted (early twentieth century).

2. England—leaf detail; painted (early twentieth century).

3. England—daisy and leaf detail; painted (early twentieth century).

4. England—rose detail; painted (early twentieth century).

5. England—corner motif detail; painted (early twentieth century).

1

2

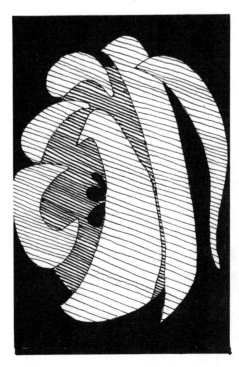

3

4

5

6. England—rose and leaf detail by Frank Nurser; painted (early twentieth century).

7. England—leaf detail from cabin block by Frank Nurser (early twentieth century).

8. England—rose detail from a cabin block by Frank Nurser (early twentieth century).

9. England—detail from a stool by Fred Winnet; painted (early twentieth century).

10. England—rose detail by Frank Jones (early twentieth century).

11. England—corner cupboard detail; painted (early twentieth century).

12. England—table cupboard detail; painted by Bill Hodgson (early twentieth century).

13. England—table cupboard detail, painted by Bill Hodgson (early twentieth century).

14. England—rose detail by George Crowshaw (early twentieth century).

15. England—daisy detail by George Crowshaw (early twentieth century).

Vases of Flowers

1. America—detail from a Pennsylvanian German candle box; painted (nineteenth century).

2. America—detail from a Pennsylvanian German dough trough; painted (nineteenth century).

3. America—detail from a Pennsylvanian German chest; painted (eighteenth century).

4. America—detail from a Pennsylvanian German chest; painted (eighteenth century).

5. America—detail from a Pennsylvanian German dower chest; painted (eighteenth century).

1

2

3

4

5

6

7

8

6. America—detail from a Pennsylvanian Polish (?) chest; painted (eighteenth century).

7. America, Lancaster County, Pa.—detail from a chest; painted (eighteenth century)

8. Polish, Mala Laka, Katowice—detail from a hope chest; painted (nineteenth century).

9. Germany—detail from an Alpine chest; painted (eighteenth century).

10. America, Connecticut—detail from a chest; painted (nineteenth century).

9

10

Fancy Flowers

1. Norway—a wooden plate; painted (early nineteenth century).

2. Norway—a bentwood box lid; painted (nineteenth century).

3. Germany, Bavaria—a detail from a small chest; (eighteenth century).

4. Germany, Bavaria—a detail from a small chest; (eighteenth century).

5. Mexico—a detail from a small chest; painted (early twentieth century).

1

2

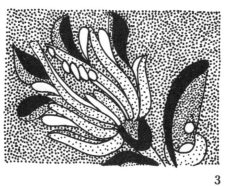

3

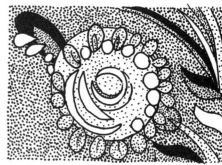

4

5

144

6

7

8

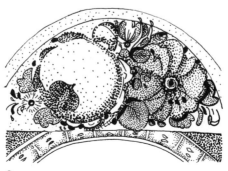

9

6. England—a canal boat corner cupboard; painted (early twentieth century).

7. England—a canal boat corner cupboard; painted (early twentieth century).

8. Germany—a clock face; painted (nineteenth century).

9. Germany—a clock face; painted (nineteenth century).

145

Trees

1. America—Pennsylvanian "Bird Tree" sculpture; worked with saw and gouge, a pierced, carved, and painted composition (early nineteenth century).

2. America, Hingham, Mass.—detail from a door panel; painted (late eighteenth century).

3. Germany, Seiffen—toy trees; turned, carved, and painted (early twentieth century).

4. Wales—detail from a love spoon handle; knife-worked, relief-carved, chip-carved, and incised (nineteenth century).

5. America, New England—detail from a fireboard; painted with sponge and brush (early nineteenth century).

2

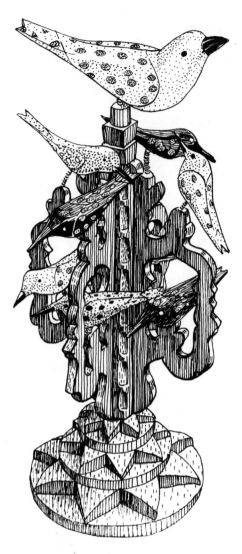

1

3

4

5

6

7

9

8

6. America, Chenango County, N.Y.—detail from a wall/panel picture; stencil-printed (early nineteenth century).

7. America, Chenango County, N.Y.—detail from a wall/panel picture; stencil printed (early nineteenth century).

8. America, New England—a stencil plate cut by William Eaton (early nineteenth century).

9. Germany, Seiffen—toy trees; knife-worked, whittled, shaved, and composite (twentieth century).

Stencil-Decorated Walls and Floors

1

2

1. America, Hampstead, N.H.—detail from a wall panel; stencil-printed (early nineteenth century).

2. America, Antrim, N.H.—detail from a wall panel; stencil-printed (early nineteenth century).

3. America, Windham, Conn.—wall panel detail; stencil-printed (early nineteenth century).

4. America, Chenango County, N.Y.—detail from an overmantel design; stencil-printed (early nineteenth century).

5. America, Athol, Mass.—by Moses Eaton, detail from a wall panel design; stencil-printed on unpainted wood (early nineteenth century).

6. America, Antrim, N.H.—by Moses Eaton, detail from a dado design; stencil-printed (early nineteenth century).

7. America, Chenango County, N.Y.—detail from a border design; stencil-printed (early nineteenth century).

3

4

5

6

7

8

9

8. America, Danvers, Mass.—detail from a floor border; stencil-printed (early nineteenth century).

9. America, Massachusetts—detail from a floor design; stencil-printed (early nineteenth century).

149

Carved Leaves and Flowers

1. Sweden, Harjedalen—sectional butter press; knife- and gouge-worked, low relief-carved, and chip-carved (nineteenth century).

2. Iceland—detail from a bed board; knife- and gouge-worked, carved in low relief with a flat ground (nineteenth century).

3. England—details from bedposts; worked with knife and gouge; deep gouge carving with incised line and undercuts (sixteenth century).

4. England, Salisbury—detail from a dole cupboard; knife- and gouge-worked, gouge-carved, and pierced (sixteenth century).

1

2

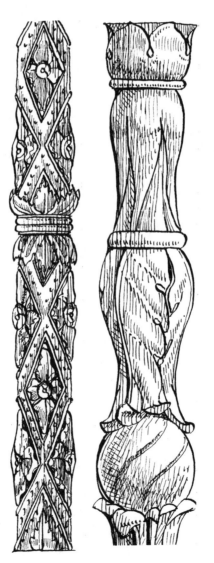

3

4

5

6

7

5. Sweden—hanging shelf/rack; knife- and gouge-worked, deep gouge carving, in the round, jointed, and painted (eighteenth century).

6. Iceland—detail from a bed board; gouge- and knife-worked, carved in shallow relief with a flat ground (nineteenth century).

7. England—detail from a court cupboard; gouge- and knife-worked, shallow relief-carved, and incised (seventeenth century).

Bronze and Gold Stencils

1. America, Conn.—detail from a venetian blind cornice; oiled card stencil plate, varnish and gold and bronze powders, painted black/blue, stencil-printed with varnish, and dusted with metallic powders (nineteenth century).

2. America, Conn.—chair rail detail, by John L Hull; oiled card stencil plate, varnish, gold, and bronze powders, painted black/blue, stencil-printed with varnish, and dusted with metallic powders (nineteenth century).

1

2

3

4

5

3. America, Robertsville, Conn.—chair rail design, oiled card stencil plate, varnish, gold, and bronze powders, painted black/blue, stencil-printed with varnish, and dusted with metallic powders (nineteenth century).

4. America, New England—chair rail design, fruit detail; oiled card stencil plate, varnish, gold, and bronze powders, painted black/blue, stencil-printed with varnish, and dusted with metallic powders (nineteenth century).

5. America, Sheffield, Mass.—by Jarred Johnson, chair rail design; oiled card stencil plate, varnish, gold, and bronze powders, painted black/blue, stencil-printed with varnish, and dusted with metallic powders (nineteenth century).

Chapter Five

Animal Forms

Ducks and Decoys

1. Sweden, Uppland—detail from a distaff; saw, sawn and fretted (nineteenth century).

2. America, Cape May County, N.J.—egret decoy; knife-worked, carved in the round, and painted (nineteenth century).

3. Poland, Kurpie—chair with duck splat detail; saw, sawn and fretted (end of the eighteenth century).

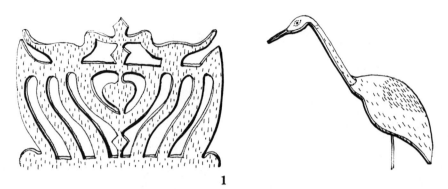

1

2

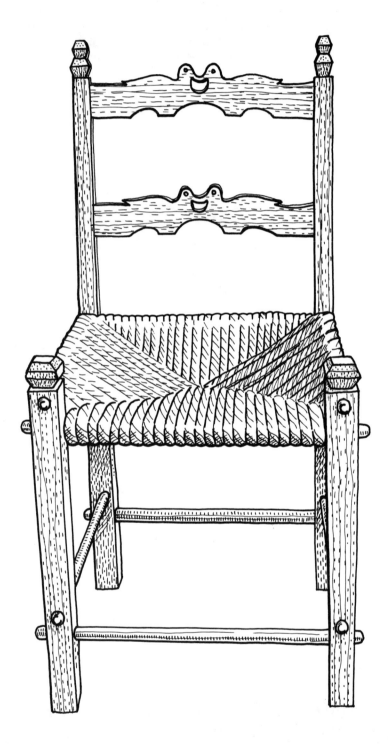

3

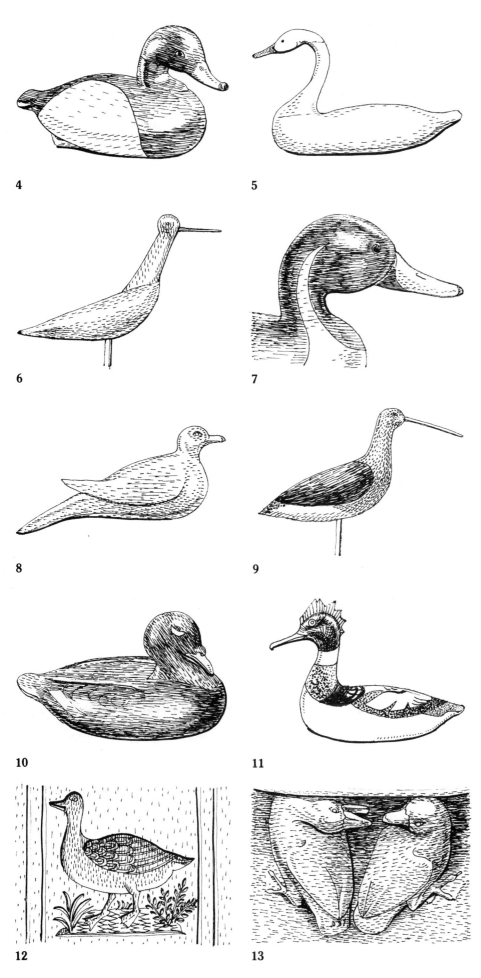

4. America, Elkton, Md.—bluebill decoy; knife-, gouge-, and saw-worked, carved in the round, knife-detailed, and painted (nineteenth century).

5. America, Havre-de-Grace, Md.—wild swan decoy; knife-, gouge-, and saw-worked, carved in the round, and painted (nineteenth century).

6. America, Nantucket Island, Mass.—a yellowleg decoy; knife-worked, whittled (nineteenth century).

7. America, Delaware Bay—pintail drake decoy detail; knife-, and gouge-worked, carved, whittled, and painted (nineteenth century).

8. America, Aiken, Md.—pigeon decoy; knife-worked, and whittled (nineteenth century).

9. America, Connecticut—shorebird decoy; knife- and gouge-worked, carved, whittled, and painted (nineteenth century).

10. America, Monhegan Island, Me.—white-winged coot decoy; knife- and gouge-worked, carved, whittled, and painted (nineteenth century).

11. America—merganser decoy; knife- and gouge-worked, carved, whittled, and painted (nineteenth century).

12. America, Pennsylvania—springerle/biscuit/gingergread mould detail; knife- and gouge-worked, carved in a shallow relief so as to give a proud/positive print (nineteenth century).

13. England, Wells Cathedral, Somerset—misericord seat detail, knife- and gouge-worked, deep undercut gouge carving (fourteenth century).

157

Painted and Stencilled Birds

1. America, Pennsylvania—chest detail; stencil-printed swan (nineteenth century).

2. America, Pennsylvania—chest detail; stencil-printed roosters (nineteenth century).

3. America, Taunton, Mass.—chest of drawers detail; painted bird (eighteenth century).

4. America, Pennsylvania—chest detail; stencil-printed eagle (nineteenth century).

5. America, Centre County, Pa.—dower chest detail; painted bird (early nineteenth century).

6. America, Pennsylvania—dower chest detail; painted bird and berries (eighteenth century).

7. America, Pennsylvania—dower chest detail; painted bird (eighteenth century).

8. America, Mahantango Valley, Pa.—desk detail; painted doves (nineteenth century).

9. America, Mahantango Valley, Pa.—detail from a small dough trough, painted (nineteenth century).

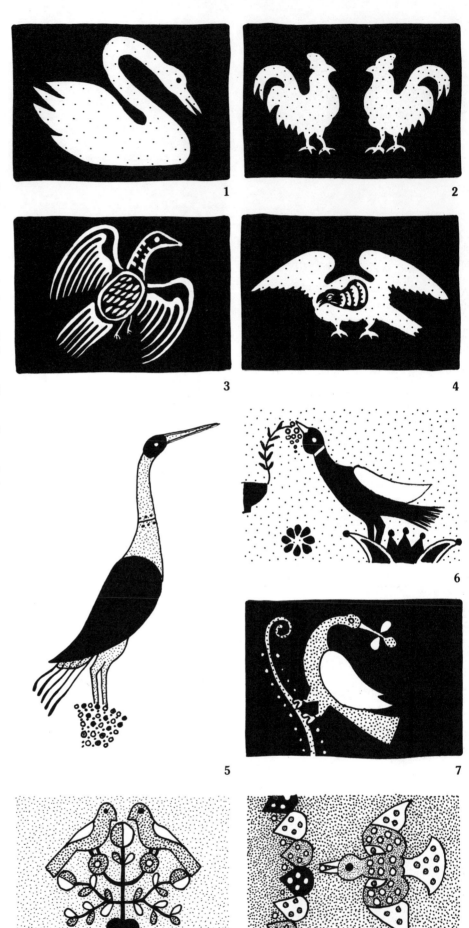

10
11
12
14
13

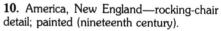

15
16
17

10. America, New England—rocking-chair detail; painted (nineteenth century).

11. America, Connecticut—tavern sign detail; painted (early nineteenth century).

12. England—by Frank Nurser, a canal boat detail; painted door (early twentieth century).

13. America, Duxbury, Mass.—overmantel by Rufus Hathaway; painted (early nineteenth century).

14. England—inn sign, Black Swan; painted (nineteenth century).

15. America—by W. P. Eaton, a chair back detail; stencil-printed (nineteenth century).

16. America—a Pennsylvanian German dower chest detail; painted (late eighteenth century).

17. America, New England—picture frame detail; stencil-printed (early nineteenth century).

Carved Birds

1. Austria, Salzburg—detail from a washing beater; knife-worked, and incised (nineteenth century).

2. Austria, Tyrol—detail from a salt box; knife-worked, incised, and chip-carved (eighteenth century).

3. England—detail from an inlaid box; saw- and knife-worked (seventeenth century).

4. Sweden, Dalarne—detail from a piece of harness; knife- and gouge-worked, carved in the round, and knife-incised (nineteenth century).

5. Germany—detail from a chair back; sawn, knife- and gouge-worked, pierced, chip-carved, and incised (nineteenth century).

6. England—detail from a confectioner's icing mould; knife- and gouge-worked, carved in shallow relief so as to give a proud/positive print (nineteenth century).

7. England, Wells Cathedral, Somerset—detail from a misericord seat; knife- and gouge-worked, deep gouge carving with undercuts and incised work (fourteenth century).

8. England—detail from a gingerbread mould; knife- and gouge-worked, carved in shallow relief so as to give a positive print/press (nineteenth century).

9. Sweden, Jamtland—a beer-goose ale vessel; knife- and gouge-worked, carved in the round, incised, and painted (eighteenth century?).

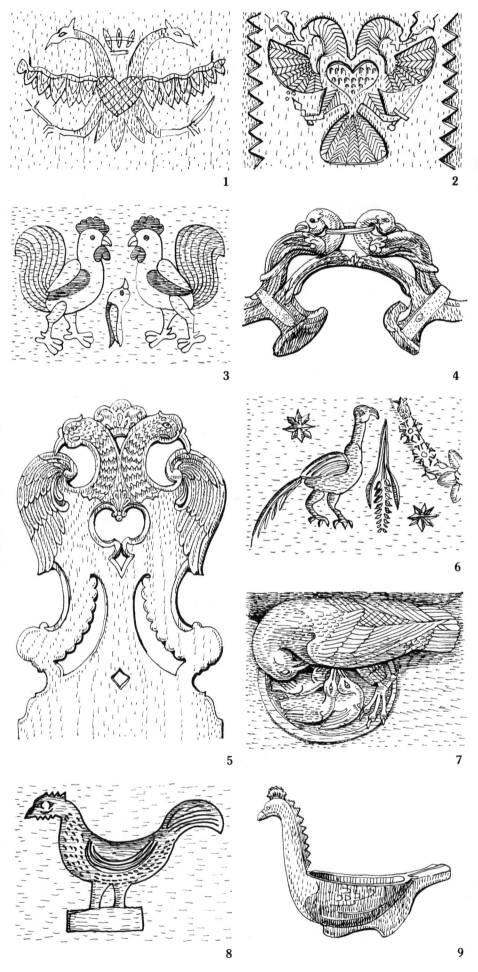

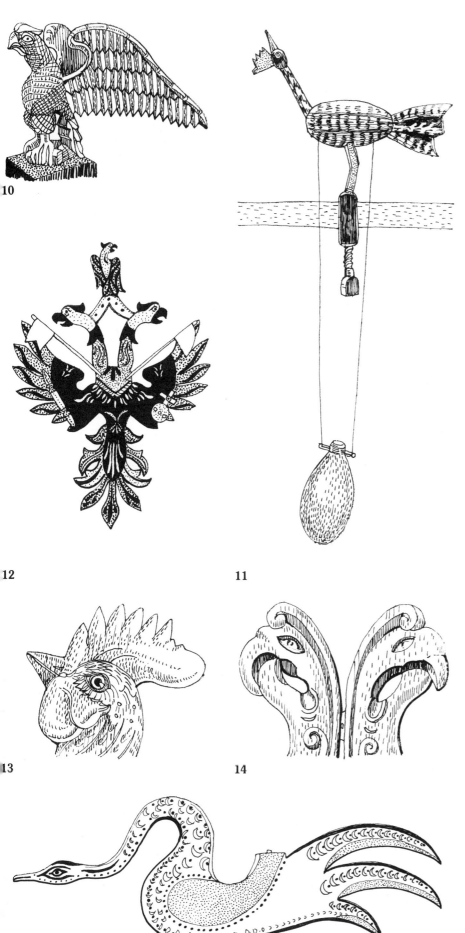

10. America—by William Schimmel, an eagle sculpture; knife- and gouge-worked, carved in the round, textured, and painted (nineteenth century).

11. America—Pennsylvanian German working toy, pendulum operated; knife- and gouge-worked, carved in the round, incised, and painted (nineteenth century).

12. Germany—a shooting target; saw- and knife-worked, fretted, and painted (nineteenth century).

13. England—a nutcracker detail; knife-worked, and whittled (nineteenth century).

14. Sweden, Smaland—horse collar detail; knife- and gouge-worked, carved in the round, and incised (nineteenth century).

15. America, Ware, N.H.—detail from a weather vane, swan (broken); knife-worked, carved, and painted (nineteenth century).

161

Birds and Beasts

1. America, Columbus, N.Y.—design from parlor wood sheathing; stencil-printed (early nineteenth century).

2. Germany—stork rider toy; turned, carved in the round, and painted (nineteenth century).

3. America, Pennsylvania—"Swan" sculpture by John Scholl; fretted, built-up, and painted (late nineteenth century).

4. America, East Harwich, Mass.—a green-winged teal; knife- and gouge-worked, carved in the round, and painted (early twentieth century).

5. America, Portland, Me.—box detail; knife- and gouge-worked, carved in the round, and incised (late nineteenth century).

6. America—stern detail from the ship *Columbia*; knife- and gouge-worked, carved in the round, incised, and painted (nineteenth century).

1

2

3

4

5

6

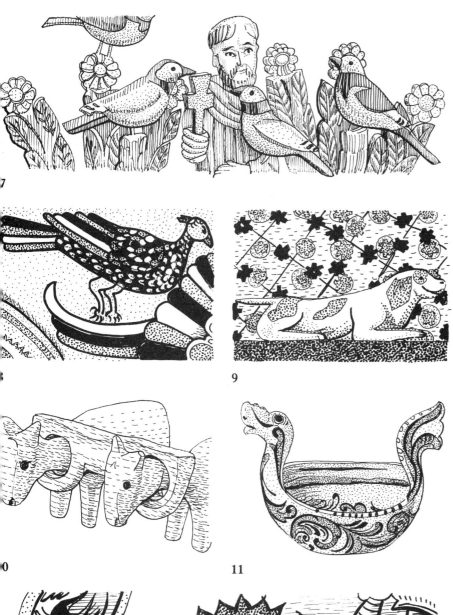

7

8

9

0

11

2

7. Poland—"St. Francis among the birds" sculpture; knife- and gouge-worked, carved in the round, and painted (nineteenth century?).

8. Russia—detail from a wine bowl; carved and painted (late eighteenth century).

9. America, Clinton, Conn.—inn sign detail; painted (early nineteenth century)

10. America—detail from a yoked oxen toy/ornament; knife-worked, and whittled (late nineteenth century).

11. Norway—drinking bowl; carved in the round, and painted (nineteenth century?).

12. Italy, Sicily—detail from a cart; painted (eighteenth century).

163

Toys

1. Germany—counterbalance toy; lathe, gouge, saw- and gouge-worked, turned, carved and painted (nineteenth century).

2. Russia—"bear and woodcutter" working toy; knife- and saw-worked, cut, whittled, and painted (nineteenth century).

1

2

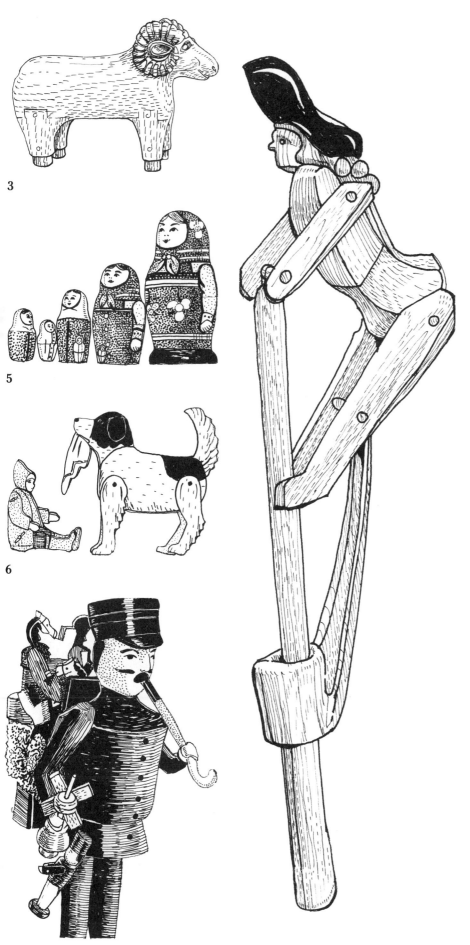

3. America—Pennsylvanian German toy ram-stool; gouge- and knife-worked, carved, jointed, and painted (nineteenth century).

4. Germany—penny fair toy, "Admiral-up-a-mast" working toy; knife-worked, whittled, and painted (nineteenth century).

5. Russia—nesting Matreshka dolls; lathe- and gouge-worked, turned, and painted (nineteenth century).

6. America—Crandall-type dog-and-child toy; fretted, jointed, and painted (early twentieth century).

7. Germany, Seiffen—"toy seller" doll; turned, carved, and painted (early twentieth century).

Masks and Fearsome Faces

1. England—nutcracker detail; knife-worked, and whittled (eighteenth century).

2. Switzerland, Lucerne—mask; knife- and gouge-worked, carved, and painted (nineteenth century?).

3. England—Punch and Judy puppet, Mr. Punch; knife-worked, whittled, and painted (nineteenth century).

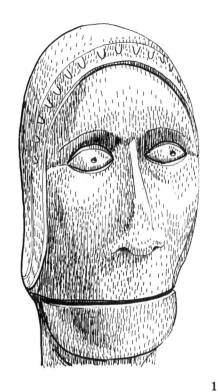

1

2

3

4

5

6

7

8

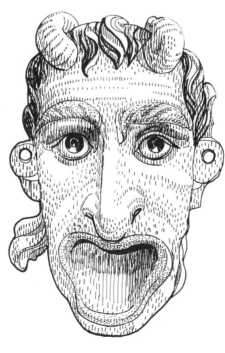

9

4. France—"old woman's tooth" router plane; knife- and gouge-worked, carved in the round (sixteenth century).

5. France, Alsace—flour spout; carved and painted (nineteenth century).

6. Holland—nutcracker; knife-worked, whittled, and pivoted/hinged (sixteenth century).

7. Germany, Tyrol—mask; carved, and painted (nineteenth century).

8. Germany, Upper Bavaria—mask; knife- and gouge-worked, carved in the round (nineteenth century?).

9. France, Alsace—flour spout; carved, and painted (nineteenth century?).

Dogs and Other Friendly Beasts

1. America, New Jersey—detail from a chest; knife-worked, and incised (seventeenth century).

2. New Mexico—chest detail; knife-worked, and incised (nineteenth century).

3. America, New England—mirror frame detail; painted and stencil-printed, gold powder and black (nineteenth century).

4. Switzerland, Canton Bern—detail from a wooden box/carrier; knife-worked, and incised (eighteenth century).

5. America—overmantel picture detail; oil painting on wood (early nineteenth century).

6. Poland—beehive; knife- and gouge-worked, carved in the round (nineteenth century).

7. England, Wells Cathedral, Somerset—detail from a misericord seat (fourteenth century).

8. England—merry-go-round board; knife- and gouge-worked, carved in deep relief, and painted (nineteenth century).

9. America, New England—trade sign detail; painted (nineteenth century).

10. England—half a butter mould, made in two halves so that a three-dimensional form could be cast/pressed, knife- and gouge-worked, carved in shallow relief (nineteenth century).

11. Germany—detail from the handle of a leatherworker's awl; knife-worked, and whittled (seventeenth century).

12. England—shop or inn sign, "The Bull"; carved, and painted (nineteenth century).

13. Poland, Silesia—ladle handle detail; knife-carved, whittled, incised, and chip-carved (nineteenth century).

14. Germany—chair back detail; pierced and carved in shallow relief (nineteenth century).

15. England—knitting sheath detail; knife-worked, and whittled (nineteenth century).

Lions and Dragons

1. Wales—love spoon detail; knife-worked, pierced, and whittled (nineteenth century).

2. America, Centre County—dower chest detail; painted (nineteenth century).

3. America, Hart, Conn.—tavern sign; painted by William Rice (nineteenth century).

4. Sweden—biscuit stamp detail; knife- and gouge-worked, shallow relief-carved, and incised (nineteenth century).

5. Sweden, Gastrikland—detail from a piece of harness; knife- and gouge-worked, carved in the round, and incised (nineteenth century).

6. Sweden, Helsingland—detail from a saddle/harness; knife- and gouge-worked, carved in the round, and incised (nineteenth century).

7. America—detail of a lion's head by John H. Bellamy; knife- and gouge-worked, carved in the round (nineteenth century).

8. England—detail from a fairground seat; knife- and gouge-worked, deeply undercut and carved in the round (nineteenth century).

9. England—detail from a misericord seat; knife- and gouge-worked, deep gouge carving, carving in the round with undercuts (fifteenth century).

10. England—detail from a misericord seat; knife- and gouge-worked, deep gouge carving, carving in the round with undercuts (fifteenth century).

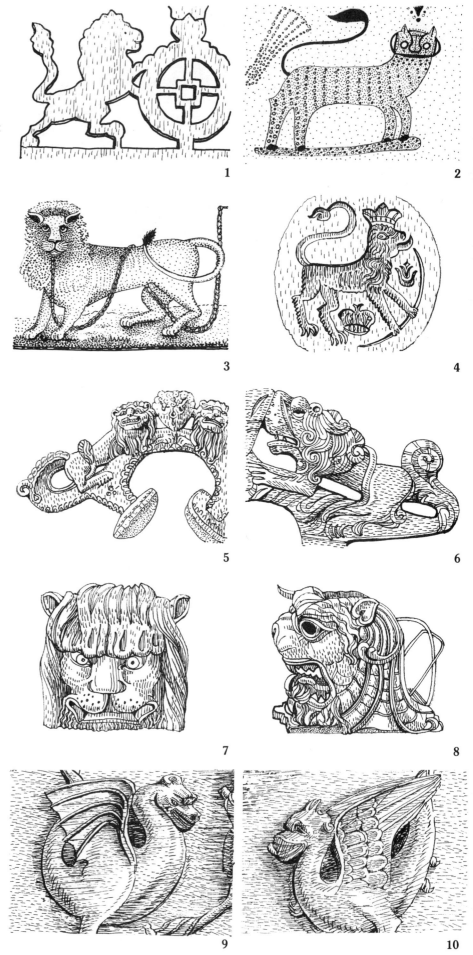

1

2

3

4

5

6

7

8

9

10

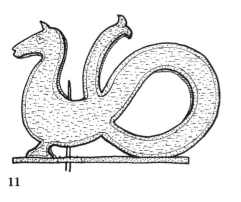

11

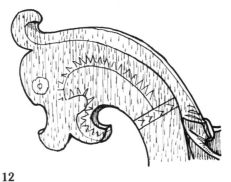

12

13

14

15

16

17

11. America, Mass.—a weather vane; saw- and knife-worked, fretted, incised, and painted (nineteenth century).

12. Sweden, Dalarne—drinking bowl detail, handle; knife- and gouge-worked, carved in the round, and incised (nineteenth century).

13. France—carved detail; knife- and gouge-worked, carved in the round, and incised (fourteenth century).

14. England—detail from a piece equipment; knife- and gouge-worked, carved in the round, and painted (nineteenth century).

15. England—church bench-end finial detail; knife- and gouge-worked, deeply gouge-carved in the round (fifteenth century).

16. England, Devon—church bench-end detail; knife- and gouge-worked, carved in deep relief with undercuts (sixteenth century).

17. England, Lincoln Cathedral—misericord detail; knife- and gouge-worked, deeply relief carved with undercuts (thirteenth century).

People Working and Playing

1. England, Cornwall—bench-end detail; knife- and gouge-worked, carved in deep relief with undercuts (sixteenth century).

2. Switzerland, Lucerne—baking mould detail; knife- and gouge-worked, carved in shallow relief, and incised (eighteenth century).

3. America, New York—fire department sign; knife- and gouge-worked, carved, and painted (nineteenth century).

4. Hungary—mirror back detail; wax inlay (nineteenth century).

1

2

3

4

5

6

5. America, Fairhaven, Mass.—weather vane for Captain David Wests' Slaughterhouse; knife-worked, carved, and painted (nineteenth century).

6. Germany—detail from a small chest; painted (eighteenth century).

7. England, King's Lynn—misencord detail, "A master carver at work"; knife- and gouge-worked, deep relief carving with undercuts (fifteenth century).

8. America, New Bedford, Mass.—shop sign "The Navigator"; knife- and gouge-worked, carved in the round, and painted (early nineteenth century).

7   **8**

173

Couples

1. Denmark—Adam and Eve detail from a hanging cupboard; knife- and gouge-worked in low relief, and painted (eighteenth century).

2. America, Pennsylvania—dower chest detail, Adam and Eve, painted (late eighteenth century).

3. England, Essex—Adam and Eve church panel detail; knife- and gouge-worked, carved in shallow relief (early sixteenth century).

4. Poland, Torun—gingerbread mould detail, Adam and Eve, knife- and gouge-worked, carved in shallow relief so as to give a positive printed/pressed image (nineteenth century).

5. England, St. Mary's Church, Newark—chair back detail, Adam and Eve; knife- and gouge-worked, deep relief carving (pre-seventeenth century, could be ancient).

1

2

3

4

5

6

7

8

6. Holland—biscuit mould detail; knife- and gouge-worked, carved in shallow relief so as to give a positive printed/pressed image (nineteenth century).

7. Iceland—box decoration; knife-, saw- and gouge-worked, pierced, carved, and painted (eighteenth century).

8. Hungary, Trans-Danubia—mirror cover detail; wax inlay (nineteenth century).

Babies and Children

1. Germany, Saxony—baby in swaddling clothes, toy; knife- and gouge-worked, carved in the round, and painted (nineteenth century).

2. America, New England—seated woman with a child, ornament; knife- and gouge-worked, deep relief carving, and painted (nineteenth century).

3. Poland, Silesia—gingerbread mould detail; carved in shallow relief so as to give a positive image when pressed/printed (nineteenth century).

4. England, Wells Cathedral, Somerset—detail from a misericord seat; knife- and gouge-worked (fourteenth century).

5. America, Virginia—oil painting on wood "The Quilting Party", detail of a boy eating an orange (eighteenth century?).

6. America, Connecticut—tavern sign detail, "A Bird in the Hand"; painted (nineteenth century).

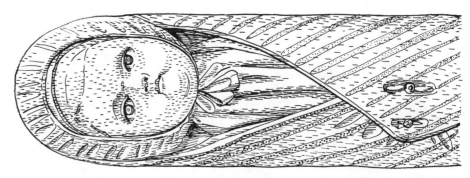

1

2

3

4

5

6

7

8

10

9

7. America, Green County, N.Y.—"William and Mary", painted by J. N. Eaton, oil painting on wood (nineteenth century).

8. America, Pennsylvania—fireboard detail, a girl in a garden; oil painting on wood (nineteenth century).

9. America—dummy board/comfort board figure, fretted, and painted (nineteenth century).

10. America, Conneticut—detail from a painted drop-leaf table; child feeding ducks, painted (nineteenth century).

177

Deer and Unicorns

1. England, Tunbridge Wells—mosaic "Tunbridge ware" lid; (nineteenth century).

2. England, St. Mary's Church, Newark—chair back detail; knife- and gouge-worked, deep relief carving (pre-seventeenth century).

3. England, Bath, Somerset—"The White Hart", inn sign; knife- and gouge-worked, carved, and painted (nineteenth century).

1

2

3

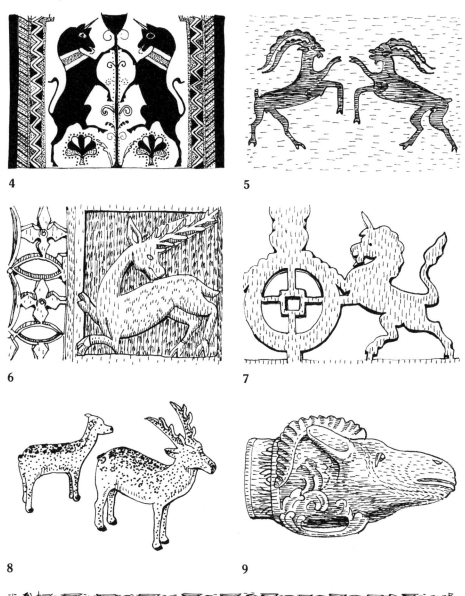

4

5

6

7

8

9

4. America, Berkshire County—dower chest detail, painted (eighteenth century).

5. Switzerland—chest detail; knife- and gouge-worked, carved shallow relief (sixteenth century).

6. France—comb detail; knife-worked, whittled, and pierced (sixteenth century).

7. Wales—love spoon detail; knife-worked, carved in shallow relief, and pierced (nineteenth century).

8. Germany—Noah's Ark animal; lathe, ring-turned, whittled, and painted (nineteenth century).

9. England—detail from a wine taster cup; knife-worked, and whittled in the round (seventeenth century?).

10. Poland, Raciborz—detail from a gingerbread mould; knife- and gouge-worked, and carved in shallow relief (nineteenth century).

10

Fairground Art

1. America, New York—Coney Island horse from the "Chafatino Carousel"; knife-, saw-, and gouge-worked, built-up, carved in the round, and painted (early twentieth century).

2. America, Philadelphia Toboggan Co.— fairgound camel; built-up, carved in the round, and painted (early twentieth century).

3. England, Burton on Trent—galloper by C. J. Spooner; built-up, carved in the round, and painted (early twentieth century).

4. England—galloper detail, carved by J. R. Anderson; built-up, carved in the round, and painted (early twentieth century).

1

2

3

4

5. Belgium—angel from a carousel; built-up, carved in the round, and painted (early twentieth century).

6. Germany—detail of a target from a throwing game; fretted, and painted (early twentieth century).

7. England—fairground spinner figure; built-up, carved in the round, and painted (early twentieth century).

8. England—dolphin car detail, carved by Fred Cox of Orton and Spooner; built-up, carved in the round, and painted (early twentieth century).

9. England—side detail from a scenic chariot ride; built-up, carved in relief, and painted (early twentieth century).

10. Germany—sleigh for a carousel, carved by W. E. Buhler; built-up, carved in relief, and painted (early twentieth century).

Carved and Painted Horses

1. America, Mahantango Valley, Pa.—detail from a miniature dough trough, painted (nineteenth century).

2. America, Wakefield, R.I.—weather vane; fretted, and painted (nineteenth century).

3. Sweden, Uppland—detail from a distaff; knife- and gouge-worked, fretted, pierced, and carved (nineteenth century).

4. America, N.Y.—weather vane for J. W. Fiske's Works; knife- and gouge-worked, carved in the round, and painted (nineteenth century).

5. England, Norwich—bench end; knife- and gouge-worked, deep relief carving with undercuts (fifteenth century).

6. Sweden, Jamtland—horse collar detail; knife- and gouge-worked, carved in the round (nineteenth century).

7. Sweden, Helsingland—detail of harness/collar; knife- and gouge-worked, carved in the round, and incised (nineteenth century).

8. Sweden, Oland—detail from a scutching knife handle; knife- and gouge-worked, carved in the round (eighteenth century).

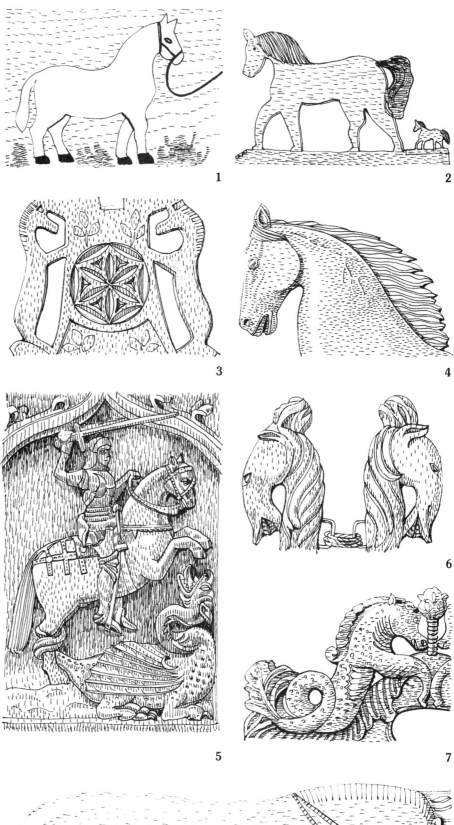

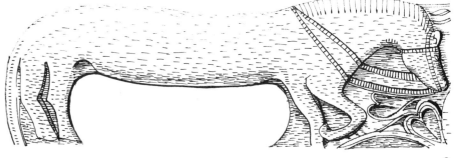

9

10

11

12

13

14

9. Russia, Arkhangelsk—detail from a distaff; painted (nineteenth century).

10. America, New England—detail from a box; stencilled (nineteenth century).

11. America—Pennsylvanian German dower chest detail; painted (eighteenth century).

12. America, Pennsylvania—trade sign detail; painted (nineteenth century).

13. Sweden, Dalarne—detail from a small cupboard; painted (nineteenth century).

14. America, Berks County, Pa.—dower chest detail; painted (nineteenth century).

Angels and Mermaids

1. America, Hingham, Mass.—weather vane; fretted and painted (nineteenth century).

2. England—detail from a chair; knife- and gouge-worked; carved, and pierced (seventeenth century).

1

2

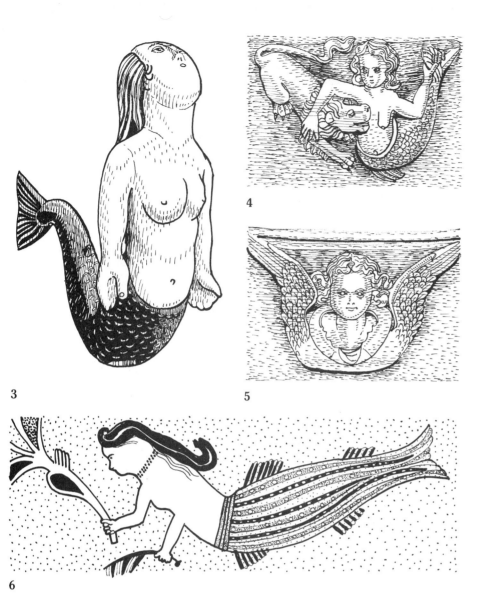

3

4

5

6

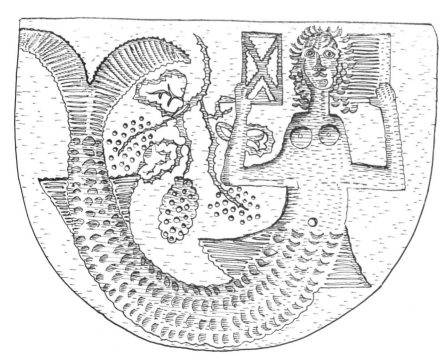

7

3. America, Baltimore, Md.—detail from a fountain; knife- and gouge-worked, carved in the round, and painted (nineteenth century).

4. England, Wells Cathedral, Somerset—detail from a misericord seat; knife- and gouge-worked, carved in deep relief with undercuts (fourteenth century).

5. England, Wells Cathedral, Somerset—detail from a misericord seat, knife- and gouge-worked, carved in deep relief with undercuts (fourteenth century).

6. America—Pennsylvanian German dower chest detail; painted (seventeenth century).

7. England, Chard, Somerset—a baker's mould; knife- and gouge-worked, carved in shallow relief so that a pressed/stamped image is positive (seventeenth century).

Female Figures in Costume

1. England—snuff peddler's shop sign/staff; carved and painted (nineteenth century).

2. England—a food mould; a fashionable lady using a churn, carved in shallow relief so as to press/stamp a positive image (eighteenth century).

3. America, New Hampshire—doll; carved in the round (eighteenth century).

4. America, Salem, Mass.—figurehead, was also used as a shop sign; gouge- and knife-worked, carved in the round, and painted (eighteenth century).

1

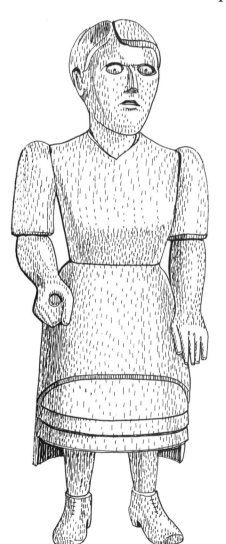

2

3

4

6

5

5. America—Miss Liberty; knife- and gouge-worked, carved in the round, and painted (nineteenth century).

6. Germany, Berchtesgaden—Jumping Jack toy; fretted, pivoted, and painted (early twentieth century).

7. America—portrait of Diantha Atwood Gordon; oil painting on wood (nineteenth century).

8. America, Calais, Me.—cigar store figure; knife- and gouge-worked, carved in the round, and painted (nineteenth century).

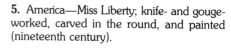

7

8

Male Figures in Costume

1. England—detail from a gingerbread mould; knife- and gouge-worked, carved in shallow relief so as to press/stamp a positive image (seventeenth century).

2. America, Lancaster County, Pa.—dower chest detail; painted (seventeenth century).

3. Denmark—detail from a cupboard; painted (nineteenth century).

4. France—gingerbread mould; knife- and gouge-worked, carved in shallow relief so as to print/press a positive image (seventeenth century).

1

3

2

4

5. England—ship's figurehead "Lord Nelson"; gouge-worked, carved in the round, and painted (nineteenth century).

6. France—ship's figurehead from the ship *Franklin*; gouge-worked, carved in the round, and painted (eighteenth century).

7. America—whirligig wearing Zouave infantry costume; knife- and gouge-worked, carved, and painted (nineteenth century).

8. America, Ohio—cigar store Indian "Seneca John" shop sign; knife- and gouge-worked, carved in the round, and painted (nineteenth century).

9. England—Jumping Jack toy; made by a sailor, carved, and painted (nineteenth century).

Index

Page numbers in boldface represent the major discussion of folk art design for each specific country.